Bake a *Business* Book

How one mum entrepreneur uses an eight-step process to cook up books in between feeding the kids

Dyan Burgess

Thank you for purchasing this book. You are one step closer to baking your book. When I am not baking my own books I am helping others bake theirs. My passion is creating independently published books so stories can be enjoyed for years to come.

Many names have been given to me over the years: Bank Johnny (working as a business banker), Boss, Sister, and Mum. My favourite one is 'The Story Curator'. Books need to be curated. They are one of the few enduring treasures that, because of the 'internet of things', can be created by anyone regardless of a person's means, ability, or age.

Welcome to my kitchen, where we will *Bake a (Business) Book*.

Free Checklist Templates

Please visit www.dyanburgess.com/resources for your FREE instant access to the checklists and templates used in this book. Whenever you see the image of a clipboard in this book you can access the resources and tools mentioned from from my website.

Major inspiration for the disciplined use of checklists in this book is from *The Checklist Manifesto* by Atul Gawande. On his website is this quote:

> *"Making the distinction between errors of ignorance (mistakes because we don't know enough), and errors of ineptitude (mistakes we made because we don't make proper use of what we know). Failure in the modern world, is really about the second of the errors."*

Bake a (Business) Book is about providing knowledge and making proper use of what we know, to avoid errors of ineptitude.

Why Bake a _Business_ Book?

This book is based on my personal experiences of the steps I have developed to turn content into an independently published book.

Beside publishing books, I'm a mad foodie. While cooking one day, the idea popped into my head: publishing a book is like baking a cake!

The following pages are the checklists and templates I have developed since 2011 while baking dozens of books to print and many more eBooks.

Each person will have their own method they want to follow and therefore the tools and methods in this book are suggestions based on my personal experiences. I have left lots of space for you to write your own notes and comments as you go to ensure your recipe, or in this case your book, turns out how you like it. This will enable you to build methods that work best for you, just as you would do with your favourite recipe book. Structuring the book in this way also allows you to keep it up-to-date and centralise your planning.

I have kept the use of words specific to the publishing industry to a minimum, but there are times when these particular words need to be used in order to correctly define the process. Where technical words are used they are in *italics* and are defined in the glossary at the end of the book.

You may consider reading the glossary first to provide a basic understanding of some of the technical words used in this book.

Let's bake a business book!

Contents

Where Do You Start?

With the analogy of baking a cake standing in for publishing a book, I have summarised the steps that I use to bake a business book in the table below. Each of these steps will then be reviewed in more detail.

Step	Baking	Publishing Terms
One p. 11	**Raw Ingredients**	**Content Collation** Gathering your content and sorting it into groups/topics to develop your process. Some of you will already know what is popular with your content, based on audience interaction.
Two p. 23	**Preparing for Baking**	**Editing** Once your content is assembled in a reasonable order, the editing process begins. You will need other people to look at your content and provide feedback.
Three p. 35	**Some Fine Print**	**The Legal Bits—Part I** This is the first stage of meeting your legal requirements.

Four p. 47	**Bake Your Book**	**Interior Design** Designing of the interior pages of your book.
Five p. 57	**Continue to Bake Your Book**	**Exterior Design** Designing the exterior of your book (the cover).
Six p. 65	**Cutting Your Cake and Sharing It Around**	**Distribution** Choosing your distribution platforms.
Seven p. 71	**More Fine Print**	**The Legal Bits—Part II** This is the second stage of meeting your legal requirements.
Eight p. 81	**Finishing up**	**Marketing** How will you market your book?

The first two steps, Content Collation and Editing, are generally the most time-consuming of all the processes. There is a good reason for this; the better the manuscript after these two steps, the easier the final stage of baking (i.e. processing to publication) will be. The remaining steps are essentially mechanical. Take it all step-by-step, process-by-process, with the legal bits mixed in. Let's look at each of these steps.

…Before We Continue

This book does not have all the answers; I remain sceptical of those writers and industry professionals who suggest they do have all the answers when it comes to publishing.

This book outlines what I have done to bake books, and what has and has not worked for me. Keep in mind that what works for me may not work for you. My examples can be a litmus test.

Some readers will only use components of this book. Others will consume it all.

The process outlined in this book is not an 'easy' solution. I don't believe there is an easy solution in publishing. However, I have tried to keep it simple. You will need to take the time to learn if you want to do this on **your terms**, and become familiar with the language of the publishing industry.

Google 'independent publishing' and you will find plenty of businesses that will help, for a price. You need to decide what you want to afford to pay.

This book will give you the foundation knowledge to speak the language of the *independent publishing industry*. This means that you can be confident when in conversation with people in the publishing industry. In turn, this confidence can help you decide what to do, what works for you, and which areas you need assistance with.

What Inspired this Book to be Written?

When people constantly ask me the same questions. I believe that this is the universe shouting at me to listen and that I need to take action. Increasingly I have been asked about independently publishing books and what I did to make it happen when I had not been in the industry before; it was obvious that I needed to write a book about the process.

I see the world through methods and systems and pictures. It seems that other people like to use these methods and systems and pictures as well.

So what has this to do with baking?

Over the last twenty years, I have constantly 'baked' people's stories, whether this meant reading financial reports for clients while working at a major Australian bank or by creating one of many iBook's (Apple Mac-based books, for those not familiar with that term) for family and friends. Book publishing seemed to be the next logical step for me. It was a natural progression in my life, with my analytical background and my love of stories, that independent publishing would become a passion for me. I love to gather the content (ingredients), put it together (mix it up), and make (bake) a book to share. Based on this, *Bake a (Business) Book* came to life.

The Time is Now!

Kids are creating multimillion dollar businesses in between homework assignments in their bedroom, while Mum and Dad cook them dinner. People are connecting in ways we have never seen before. Technology is enabling more people to realise their dreams.

Movements have started around the world to allow people to connect in real and deep ways to find leverage for those dreams and to create new opportunities for people who would never have had such opportunity before.

Examples of 'real' people making a real difference are those like Sugata Mitra with S.O.L.E. Similarly, B1G1 founded by Masami Sato, and Thank You Water founded by three young Australians. These people are making real differences across the globe, with ideas that were not considered remote possibilities as little as ten years ago. They have connected people from all parts of the world in ways that mean that those who want to give can give and those in need can be helped in ways that they want. Providing help with clean water and education, organisations such as B1G1 and Thank You Water allow you to track exactly where your giving goes. These opportunities are creating wonderful stories about the ways we create connections and provide real help across the world.

The time is now to connect, to give, and to share by taking the stories out of our heads and independently publishing them.

Bake a (Business) Book and its processes are not about becoming the next J.K. Rowling or James Patterson. This book is about guiding or inspiring you to record your story, position your brand, and create your legacy for future generations so you can share and connect with the world.

Overview of the Business
Book Publishing Process

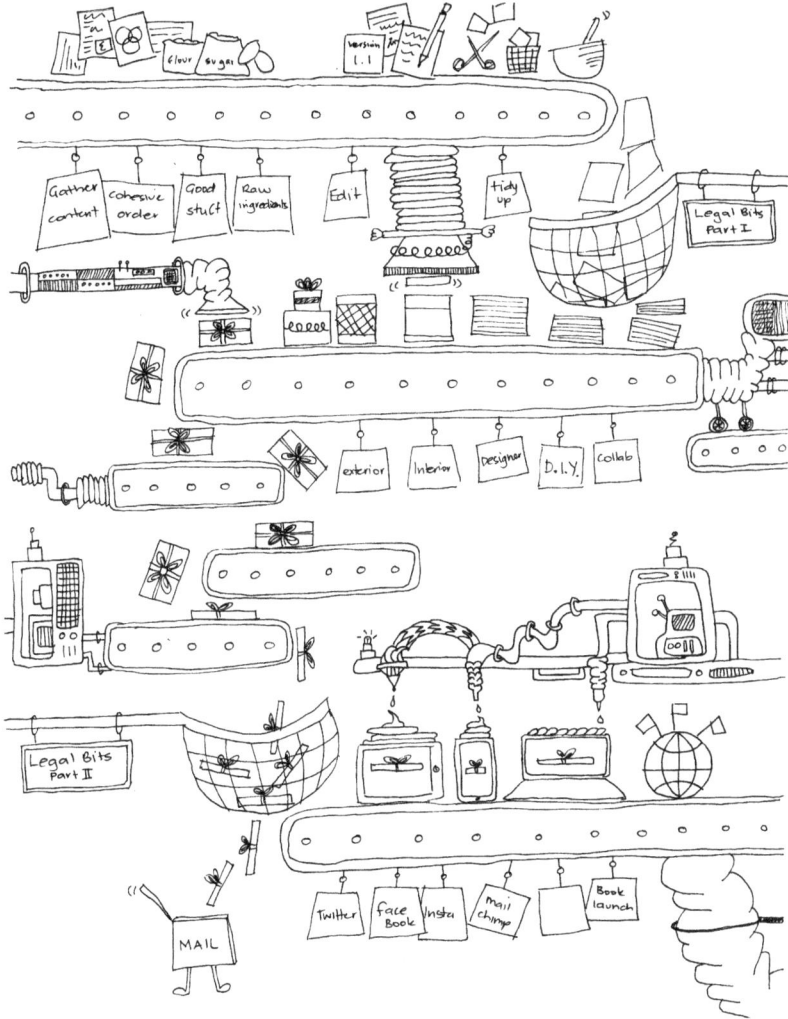

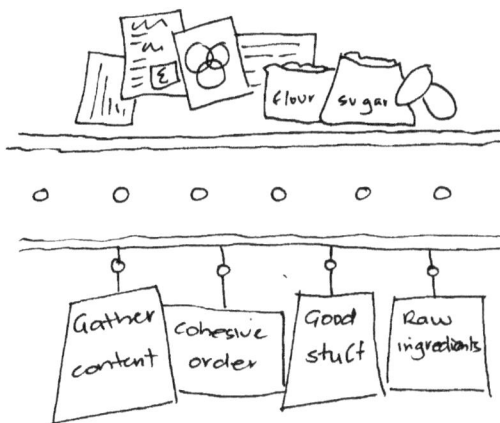

Step

1

RAW INGREDIENTS
(CONTENT COLLATION)

COLLATING YOUR CONTENT INTO AN ORGANISED FORMAT (OR ORGANISED CHAOS)

Gather Your Raw Ingredients

As with baking a cake, high quality raw ingredients are more likely to result in a high quality cake, assuming you bake it correctly. Similarly, great content + great manuscript = great book.

Tools

a. Pencil (favourite of Roald Dahl) or pen

b. Paper

c. Notebook (I love Moleskine notebooks—the grid version)

d. Word processor (for example, Microsoft Word)

e. Typewriter (favourite of Nick Cave)

f. Dictaphone (I use an app on my iPhone for this)

g. Transcriptionist (many times my personal transcriptionist www.jessetranscriptions.com has saved my sanity)

h. Internet access

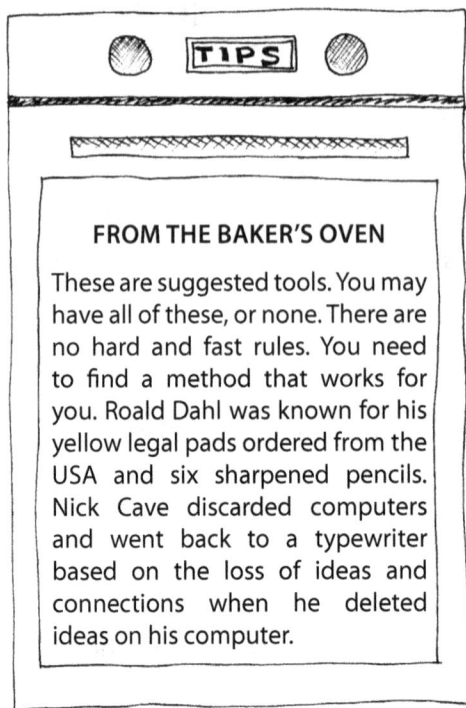

FROM THE BAKER'S OVEN

These are suggested tools. You may have all of these, or none. There are no hard and fast rules. You need to find a method that works for you. Roald Dahl was known for his yellow legal pads ordered from the USA and six sharpened pencils. Nick Cave discarded computers and went back to a typewriter based on the loss of ideas and connections when he deleted ideas on his computer.

How Can You Collate Your Content if You Don't Know Where to Start?

The first question to ask is, 'What content have I have already produced?' Consider what content you have already developed; e.g., standardised responses to clients; blog posts; interviews; articles you have written for publications, magazines, or other printed media (sometimes you will need permission to use these).
What content is sitting on your website or sitting in a filing cabinet from mail-outs, newsletters, or work from previous customers? Collect all of this information together.

The next step is to batch your content into similar themes/ categories/topics. Then you can analyse where you need to add or remove content and what seems to be a logical order for your text to be arranged in. Is your book *The Five Steps* … or *7 Ways to* … or *101 Hints and Tips for*…?

Questions to ask yourself could be:

- What is the goal of your content and your book?

- Who is your audience?

- What solution does your content offer the reader or user?

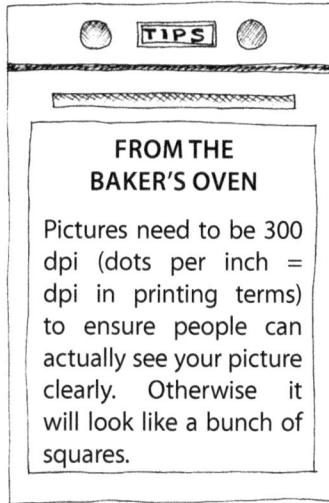

TIPS

FROM THE BAKER'S OVEN

Pictures need to be 300 dpi (dots per inch = dpi in printing terms) to ensure people can actually see your picture clearly. Otherwise it will look like a bunch of squares.

Understanding these questions will simplify your content structure. These questions will also assist to produce your introduction and conclusion. The theory here is that if you know your goal, your introduction and conclusion will write themselves … not quite, but you will have a very good sense of where to start and where to go. A basic content structure can be formed from this process.

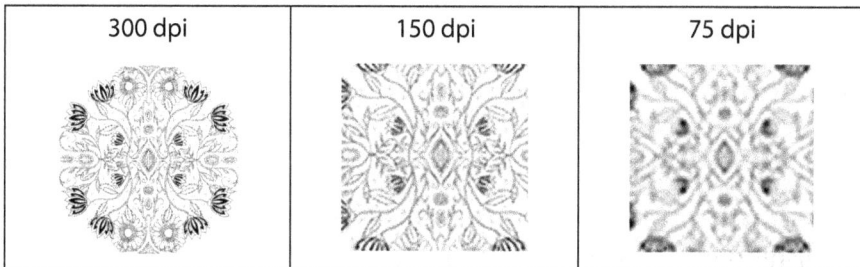

300 dpi	150 dpi	75 dpi

An editor can create a style guide to standardise the formatting adopted throughout your book, for example, the style chosen for the bullet point and numbering. The earlier in the process a style guide can be determined, the easier later steps will become. Perhaps you already have a style guide for your brand—this is a great starting point. The style guide for this book is tabled below:

Style Guide	
With the tools list	No full stops for, e.g.: 1. Upwork 2. Professional editor 3. Help forums
When there is a section entitled 'Tips from the Baker's Oven'	Box like an oven drawn around the tips
Checklists	To be created in a checklist format
Checklist Steps	No full stops as per the tools list
When the word is in italics it needs to be defined in the glossary	Check that all words are defined and that italics has been consistently applied
Typefaces	
Paragraphs	Myriad Pro Regular 12 point
Main Headings	Myriad Pro Bold 14 point
Subheading	Myriad Pro Bold 14 point
Step Numbering	Castellar MT Regular 72 Point
Spacing	Six hard returns between questions on Notes pages

When naming fictitious characters, have a list of the names and their key characteristics in a table so that characters can be differentiated easily. Otherwise you can forget who is who while protecting identities for privacy.

You need to ensure *version control*. Your sanity will be kept or lost based on your ability to keep track of your versions. This is extremely important. The goal here is to have your content (remember the publishing industry may say *manuscript*) in an organised format to provide a great foundation for your book. The better the *manuscript* is before submitting to the editor and designer, the better—even if you are the editor and designer. (I highly recommend someone else read your work. It is extremely difficult to see your own mistakes.)

Consider your experience and whether you need editing and proofreading or whether you will go straight to the book designing stage. Again, views are varied on this. Personally, I need at least one other person (ideally two or three) to check my work.

My personal experience is that the clearer you are about your thoughts, the better the result in the long run. Others reviewing your content best achieve this clarity.

"Measure twice. Cut once."

—Proverb

Method

The checklist for these steps and a Quick User Guide in Appendices A and B.

Following are the suggested steps for developing and refining your *manuscript*. The aim is to provide a coherent *manuscript* for easier transition to the next stage in your baking.

1. Review your manuscript in the following steps:
   a. Big picture/overall look: Flick through the pages. Does the style flow; are your headers and footers consistent?
   b. Pages: Are pages correctly separated?
   c. Paragraphs: Is the style consistent? How many spaces do you have?
   d. Sentences: Grammar check in Microsoft Word can be a good start.
   e. Words/typos: Again use of Microsoft Word spell check is a good starting point; ensure you choose correct language for English (e.g. UK).
2. Formatting: Get into the detail here. Have you used the same style bullet points, are your quotes consistently styled?

Setting up a checklist or table of your styles/formatting can assist to ensure consistency.

3. Consistent *typeface* for entire manuscript. Most book designers can adjust if needed. However in my experience there are less likely to be errors or confusion if this is clear from the outset.
4. Chapters to be *hyperlinked* to contents page (this is optional as some designers prefer to do the contents page links themselves).
5. Confirm your *author bio* is up to date. When was the last time you checked your details and your picture? Your *author bio* needs to be congruent with who you are and what you look like now, not twenty years ago. Please, no airbrushing. It is very confusing, particularly if you are a public speaker or regularly present to your audience.
6. *Blurb* (the text on the back cover) is also a great way to refine the pitch of your book. Some would suggest you get this right first. Interestingly, well-known children's author Emma Walton Hamilton, notes the importance of this when marketing your book.
7. Acknowledgements and thank yous. Work out the list of people who have been there for you and helped you along the way so far. You can always add more names as they arise.
8. Format to be how you want the final version i.e. new chapter, new page. Again, this assists the editor and designer to understand your thoughts and provides a clear flow of text throughout the book.
9. Headers on interior pages of book: book title LHS (left hand side) and chapter title RHS (right hand side) this is my personal preference.
10. Complete all aspects of *Document Review Checklist (Appendix C)*.
11. Consider further reviews by friends, family, and local and overseas resources.

TIPS

FROM THE BAKER'S OVEN

I cannot over-emphasise the benefits of checklists. Jim Collins's book *Great By Choice* looks at the success of the IMAX crew filming of Mt. Everest and their use of checklists, even when they had practiced their routine hundreds of times.

A checklist does not remove the need for common sense, however a checklist can save you from repeating poor choices and help to promote good choices and better systems for you (it may also help save your sanity).

For your free checklists, go to
www.dyanburgess.com/resources

NOTES:

Why do I want to write a book?

Where can I collect content?

Do I write a blog?

Have I written content for publications?

Do I have content in written form that can be scanned, converted to Word, and used as part of my book?

What is my conclusion?

What is the goal of my book?

Who is my audience?

What solution does my content offer the reader or user?

What is my blurb?

What other notes do I need to make?

What is my introduction?

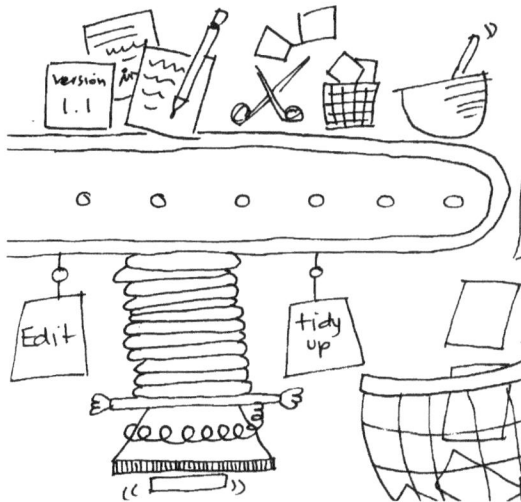

Step

2

PREPARING FOR BAKING
(EDITING)

EDITING YOUR CONTENT

You have gathered your raw ingredients. Next you need to prepare those ingredients for your recipe.

In publishing terms, preparing your raw ingredients is the editing of your *manuscript*. This step sees your key tool as people power—you will need to choose whom you will collaborate with. Who do you know that could assist in providing more content or removing content? Some of us are dot point types, while others can be verbose. Somewhere in between is probably a good balance.

> *"e n'ai fait celle-ci plus longue que parce que je n'ai pas eu le loisir de la faire plus courte." (I would have written a shorter letter, but I did not have the time.)*
>
> —Blaise Pascal

Tools

a. Upwork (formerly Elance) I have used this freelance platform for ten years: www.upwork.com

b. The Institute of Professional Editors Limited (IPED): http://iped-editors.org/

c. Writers' centre in your state or territory (Australian Society of Authors/ASA lists these writers' centres on their website https://www.asauthors.org/writers-centres)

d. Family (helps when you have academics)

e. Friends (hhmmm, this can be a double-edged sword)

f. Business associates

g. Clients (especially if you want it to be relevant to them)

h. Forums

How Long Should My Book Be?

The answer depends on your intention for your book. Hopefully, you have a rough idea on this, based on the introduction, conclusion, and blurb you worked up in the last step.

There are practical limitations on the minimum and maximum pages and file sizes for printing. Experience has taught me that a book with more than 280 pages (total weight over 500gms) becomes too bulky and more expensive to post. There can be issues with the stability of the spine with *perfect bound* books with large page numbers. Other binding methods are generally too expensive to consider when starting out.

For example, *CreateSpace* (who I use for my *print-on-demand* [POD] *paperback* production) has a minimum page number of twenty-four and maximum page number ranging from 200 to 828 (depending on the *trim* size of your book), while the maximum file size is 400MB (current as at November 2015). These file size restraints change; please check again before you proceed further.

You would also need to consider your computer's capacity and Internet connection. Files over 100MB can take quite some time to move from place to place and that can become frustrating. You want to minimise your excuses for not completing your project, so look for ways to make progress easier and success a reality.

Practically, if your book is a *paperback* it is preferable to contain sufficient pages to create a *spine* that is wide enough for your *title* and name to be printed on it. Generally, this is at least 130 pages. However, you don't want to just fill for filling's sake. This will undermine the message of the book to your audience.

How Long Should I Spend on Editing and Refining?

You want your story shared. You can become quickly sidetracked with lots of advice about methods to take. You need to decide what works for you. If you find that you are taking more than, say, two months to progress your book to the next step, I recommend you pay someone to get you moving along.

SHIP. SHIP. SHIP.

(For those not familiar with this term, it is regularly used by thought leader and bestselling author Seth Godin. See www.sethgodin.com. It means 'get it done'.)

TIPS

FROM THE BAKER'S OVEN

Some in the industry will suggest that friends and family are not a good resource. You are the best judge of your circumstances. One downside I found with family's and friends' reviews was that they knew me, so my stories needed less explaining; however that does not assist people who don't know me. It meant that, at times, my story was unclear, and people who know you won't necessarily see this. Your story needs to be clear for everyone. Family and friends, however, were great to use to find typographical and grammatical errors (any remaining errors are my own!).

Method

Prior to sending work to an editor I apply the checklist in Appendix C. Once that is applied I utilise the checklist in Appendix D which is noted below:

1. Submit manuscript to editor for them to quote their price.
2. Editor to provide a sample chapter to confirm style and all changes in *Redline* (also known as *Track Changes*).
3. Accept/reject editing from editor.
4. Editor then to work on entire book (need to ensure original sample provided is included into the full version of the final manuscript).
5. Review/approve/decline *tracked changes*. Ensure date and version number are included on your file name—for example, '150828 v3 Book Title.docx'—where the year, month, and date are the first number of the file name. Allows for easier tracking later.
6. Provide feedback.
7. Review/approve.
8. Save final version with the wording 'FINAL' in the file name. This file is then provided to the book designer.

These steps will assist you to keep your manuscript on track. I learnt the hard way with some of these steps. For example, I contracted an editor who did not use *Track Changes*, and another one who did not put the sample first chapter into the final fifteen-chapter document.

So how do you get a quote from an editor? Where do you find an editor? In the tools list I refer to my preferred resources, which are Upwork (formerly Elance) and writers' centres in your state.

You will meet people along the way and start to build more contacts.

Hang on—were you lost there with some technical terms?

What is Track Changes (or Redline Amendments)?

This is a system very familiar to those in the publishing and legal industries. *Track Changes* is a function in Microsoft Office Word and allows you to see when you, or others, have made amendments in a Word document. This tool is extremely powerful. If you are not already familiar with this tool in Word, I strongly suggest you take time to understand it. Working with someone else on your manuscript can become confusing very quickly if you don't use this tool. Your brain will be overwhelmed trying to remember what your overall plan is or was.

If anyone you are looking to work with says they don't use *Track Changes* or they don't know what *Redline* is, thank them for their time and walk away.

Where do you find Track Changes?

Below are screenshots of the menu options that you generally see in your word processing program when selecting 'Track Changes'.

Option One

1. Go to the Review tab

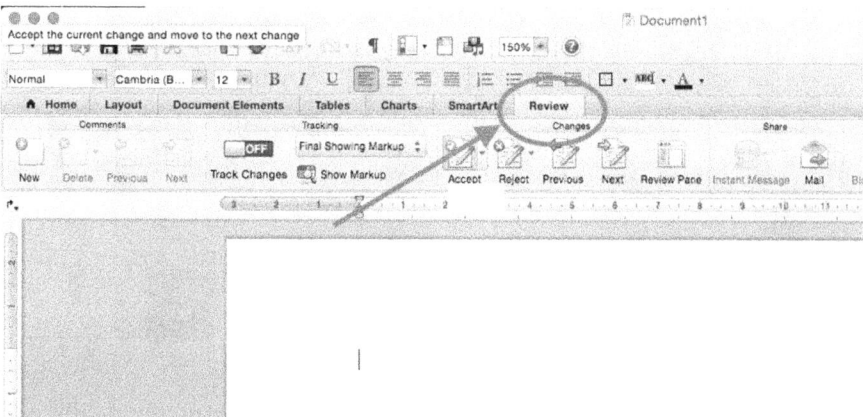

1

2. Click on the button next to the words 'Track Changes' to 'On'

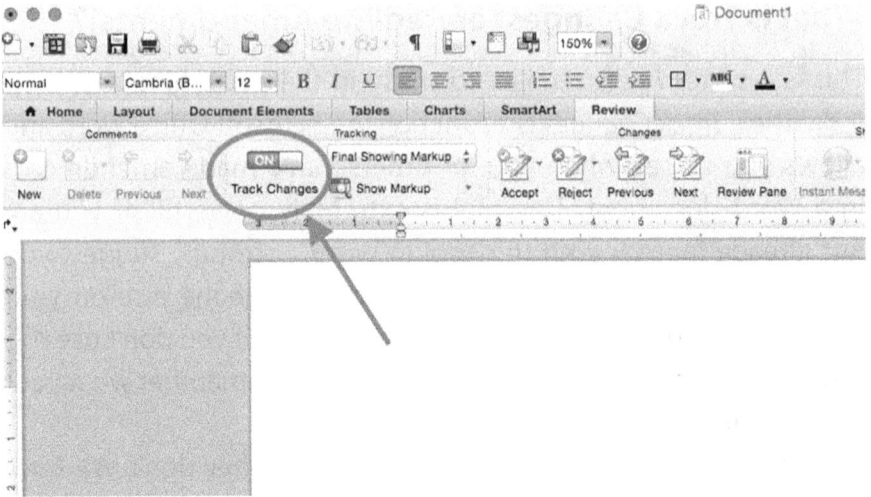

2

Option Two

1. Go to the 'Tools' menu

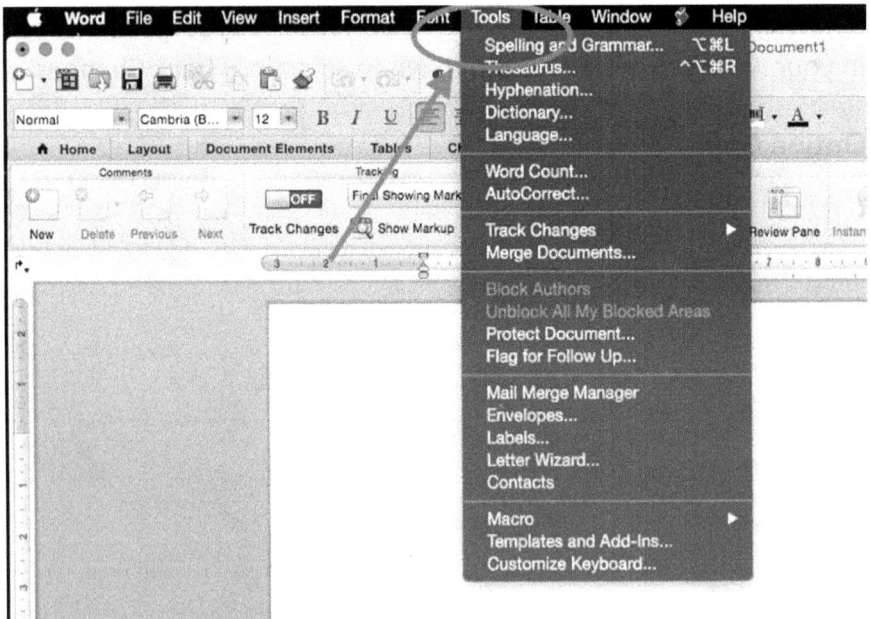

1

2. Move down to the option 'Track Changes'

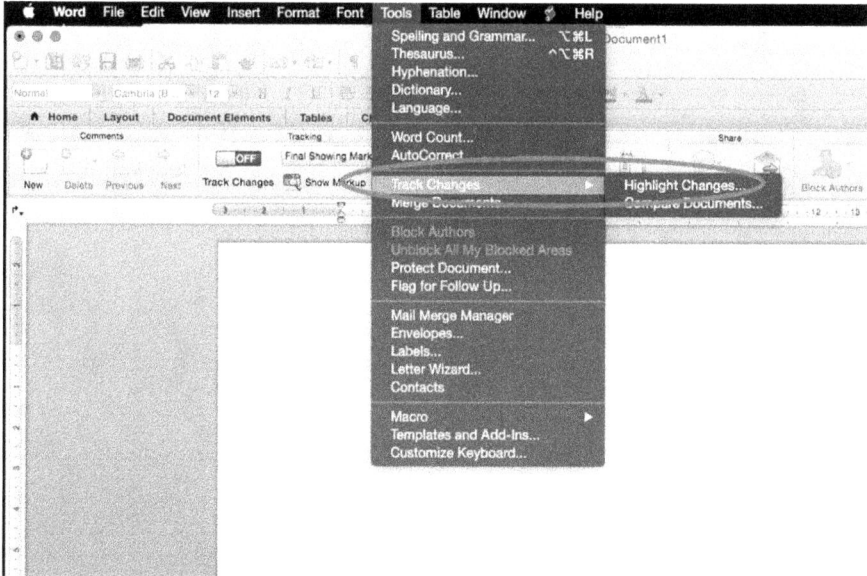

2

3. Choose 'highlight changes'

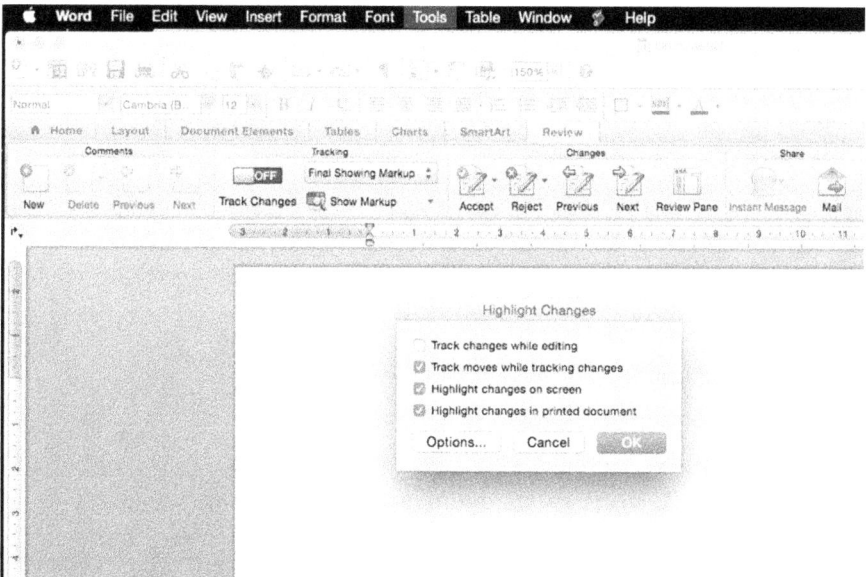

3

4. Choose options that suit you

5. Your changes will now be tracked.

For your free checklist, go to
www.dyanburgess.com/resources

NOTES:

Who will I collaborate with?

Do I need more or less content?

Who can read my manuscript and provide relevant feedback?

How long should my book be?

Where will I find my editor?

How will I ensure I am shipping at each and every step of the process?

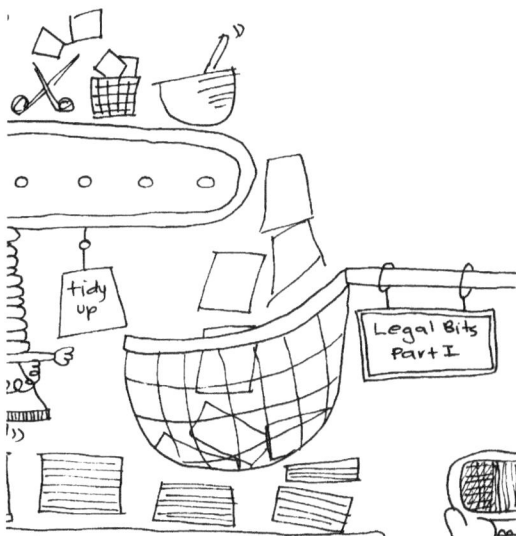

Step

3

SOME LEGAL BITS
(ISBNS AND CATALOGUING)

SOME OF THE LEGAL BITS

In cooking, this would be understanding some of the technical aspects of a recipe. Some people are not interested in the more technical aspects of cooking and the same applies with independent book publishing.

This step is part of the administration of your book. Many authors are not interested in being involved in these processes. The focus for many authors is the production of the *manuscript*. As with great cake baking, you don't need to create a four-tier cake to impress others; you can do just as well with a great chocolate ganache. Similarly, the focus needs to be on your strengths as an author, not as an administrator. Some authors can do all of these steps without a fuss. Know what you are able to do, but also be aware of what you cannot do and find others to assist.

With the growth of independent publishing, there are a number of businesses that can assist with the administration of these mechanical steps of book publishing. Again this will be defined by your budget and how much time can you spend on learning these mechanical steps.

I have a natural curiosity in pulling things apart, so I took the time to understand these processes. Once I understood them I did not want to be the one inputting the data. I created a process and trained others to do this.

If you do not want to be involved in the processing of the legal bits, this is where your tools are used as noted in Step 2. Alternatively, I have worked with various specialist independent publishing houses to assist with these processes. Google is your best resource for additional information in this space.

If you want to do these legal steps by yourself—that is, get into the technical details—then read on.

ISBN and Cataloguing

Because of the changing pace of technologies and digital systems, I am limiting the step-by-step detail for inputting data into various platforms based on the high probability that the systems will have changed at the time of or soon after the publication of this book. Showing all the steps via screen shots and web links would make it more complicated to follow the procedures, as they would be unlikely to match the current platform set up.

The main point of this process is to know what information you need, before you sit down in front of your computer. This will save you time and frustration.

I have consistently found, with almost all platforms I use, that if you know the information that is required before you sit down, generally, following the instructions on screen is straightforward. Again, there are people who spend hours perfecting and sharing tutorials on YouTube, so use Google, or look at programs offered by the platform you are using for the most up-to-date *dashboard* hints and tips.

ISBN Application

You will need to create an account with Thorpe Bowker (www. thorpebowker.com.au). You can purchase single or bulk lots of ISBNs. On the basis that an ISBN is required for each format/style of book, you can often need three ISBNs for one book. That is because you'll typically produce several versions, e.g. paperback, hardback, eBook, and so it is best to buy a batch of ten numbers rather than one.

An ISBN is defined as International Standard Book Number.

Appendix E provides a sample table to track ISBN's.

I keep a centralised tracking table for the allocation of ISBNs so that I can easily reference which ISBN belongs to which book title and format. A sample of a tracking table is in Appendix E.

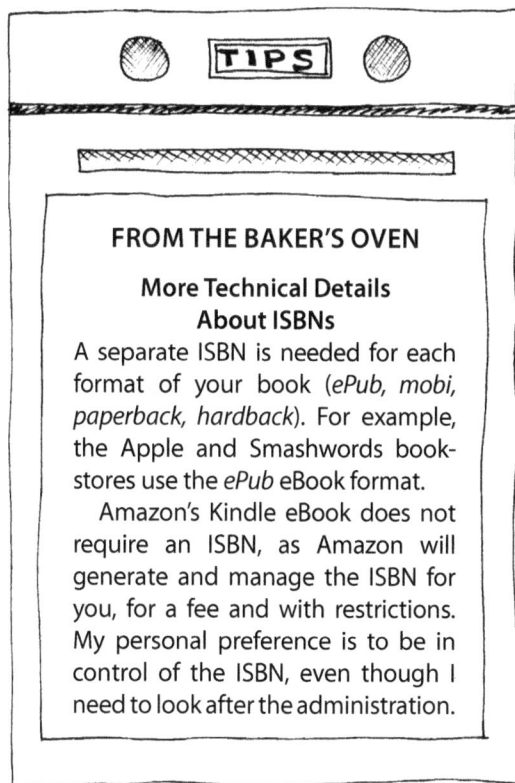

FROM THE BAKER'S OVEN

More Technical Details About ISBNs

A separate ISBN is needed for each format of your book (*ePub, mobi, paperback, hardback*). For example, the Apple and Smashwords bookstores use the *ePub* eBook format.

Amazon's Kindle eBook does not require an ISBN, as Amazon will generate and manage the ISBN for you, for a fee and with restrictions. My personal preference is to be in control of the ISBN, even though I need to look after the administration.

Once an ISBN is assigned to a *title*, you need to register the book on the *My Identifiers* website. Here are the steps to register on myidentifiers.com.

Step 1:   Gather information as per '*My Identifiers Checklist*' (Appendix F) referring to your source material.

Step 2:   Submit registration to My Identifiers.

Practical steps for the website input are as follows:

Step 1:   Log into www.myidentifiers.com.au with the username and password.

Step 2:   Go to the 'My Account' tab and select 'Manage ISBN'.

Step 3:   Select the ISBN from the list or enter the ISBN in the search box.

Step 4: Click on 'Assign Title'.

Step 5: Open 'My Identifiers Checklist'.

Step 6: Go back to My Identifiers web page and insert the following information:
- Title
- Subtitle, if any
- Description
- Publication date
- Copyright year

Step 7: Once all the required fields are entered, upload the image of the cover. This step can be done later.

Step 8: Upload the manuscript.

Step 9: Click on 'Save' and 'Go to Contributor'.

Step 10: On the 'Contributor' section, enter the following information:
- Contributor entity (person or company)
- First and last name
- Enter the author's bio

Step 11: Click 'Save' and go to 'Format and Size'.

Step 12: On the 'Format and Size' page, select the 'Medium Type' (digit, print, eBook, etc.).

Step 13: Select the formatting type (A4, 46 size, etc.).

Step 14: Packaging description (binding, clamshell, slip case, etc.).

Step 15: Select the size.

Step 16: Select title volume number.

Step 17: Click 'Save' and go to 'Sales and Pricing'.

Step 18: On the 'Sales and Pricing' section, enter info about where the title is sold.

Step 19: Enter title status.

Step 20: Enter publication date.

Step 21: Enter target audience.

Step 22: Enter age group.

Step 23: Next go to 'Country Price Data' section and select currency.

Step 24: Enter price type and price discounted code.

Step 25: Next go to 'Country Additional Sales Information' section and select title ship date.

Step 26: Enter 'On Sale and Final Return Date' or 'Out of Print Date'.

Step 27: Next go to 'Country Series Title and Series Volume Number'.

Step 28: Next go to 'Country Sales Right Information' and enter sales right type.

Step 29: Enter sales right country or rights territory.

Step 30: Click 'Submit'.

Cataloguing-in-Publication Application

Once a manuscript has been finalised and an ISBN has been assigned, then you can submit your book for *Cataloguing-in-Publication (CiP)* on National Library of Australia's website.

Why Apply for Cataloguing-in-Publication?

This step puts your book into the National Library of Australia catalogue. This allows your work to be found via the library's 'Trove' program, which is used by the publishing industry.

How to Submit Cataloguing-in-Publication

Cataloguing-in-Publication (CiP) is a free service offered to publishers by the National Library of Australia to provide a catalogue record for publications that have not yet been published. Please note the following before you apply for a *CiP* entry:

1. A valid Australian ISBN is required before proceeding with this form. Allow ten working days (Mon-Fri excluding public holidays) for your application to be processed.

2. Once an ISBN is assigned to a title, you can register the book on National Library of Australia's website. An example of a checklist is provided in Appendix G and a blank checklist is provided in Appendix H.

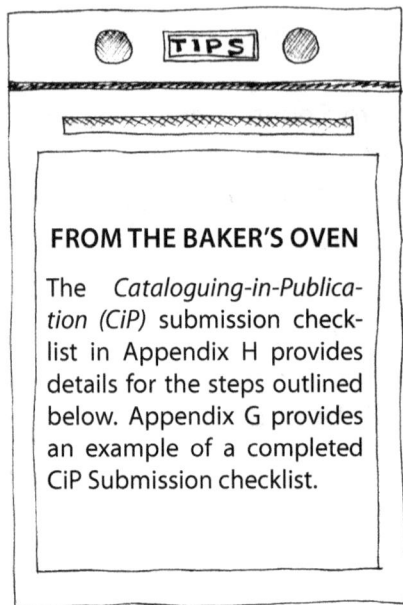

FROM THE BAKER'S OVEN

The *Cataloguing-in-Publication (CiP)* submission checklist in Appendix H provides details for the steps outlined below. Appendix G provides an example of a completed CiP Submission checklist.

Utilising the example and template checklists to gather your data before logging into the National Library website will save you time and confusion.

Steps to submit your book details for *CiP* registration are below:

Step 1:   Log in to http://www.nla.gov.au/cip.

Step 2:   Click on 'Apply for *CiP* entry'.

Step 3:   Go to 'Publisher Contact Details' by entering the following information in the fields.

Step 4:   Enter publisher name, e.g. 'Daniel Jones'.

Step 5:   Enter category, e.g. 'Individual'.

Step 6:   Enter address.

Step 7:   Enter phone number.

Step 8:   Enter fax number (if you have one).

Step 9: Enter email address.

Step 10: Enter contact name.

Step 11: Contact details consent, e.g. 'Yes'.

Step 12: Enter title.

Step 13: Enter subtitle.

Step 14: Enter edition. If there is an edition or revision number, revised publication will be Edition 2; otherwise it will be first edition (Edition 1).

Step 15: Enter imprint, e.g. 'Daniel Jones'. An imprint can mean a trade name under which a work is published. One single publishing company may have multiple imprints; the different imprints are used by the publisher to market works to different demographic consumer segments. For example, under Simon & Schuster, there are four imprints: Pocket Books, Scribner, The Free Press, and Simon Pulse. If this situation is not applicable to your company, please input 'as above' or fill with your company name.

Step 16: Enter Format 1, e.g. 'Paperback'.

Step 17: Enter ISBN.

Step 18: Enter retail price.

Step 19: Enter system requirements, e.g. PDF.

Step 20: Select planned date of publication.

Step 21: Select month of publication.

Step 22: Enter author/contributor information. Enter the full author statement exactly as it appears on the title page, including all authors, editors, illustrators, etc. and any words indicating their roles or functions. Only those listed on the title page are included in catalogue records e.g. 'By John Citizen; photographs by J. R. Bloggs; edited by J. Smith; prepared under the direction of Smith Corporation'.

Step 23: Life dates/middle names of authors/contributors. List contributors including year of birth or middle name to help distinguish between persons of the same name. Please ensure that contributors consent to this information appearing in the CIP record. (E.g. Jo M. Bloggs, 1952.)

Step 24: What is this publication about? Describe the main topics and themes of the work, including relevant geographic places, subjects, and names of people and organisations, including the name of the subject of a biography.

Step 25: Enter genre of publication.

Step 26: Enter primary audience.

Step 27: Enter series title. If the publication is part of a series, provide the title of the series, exactly as it will appear, and any applicable series numbering.

Step 28: Enter series numbering (e.g. Vol. 3 no. 7).

Step 29: Enter Series ISSN.

Step 30: Bibliography/index.

Step 31: Multivolume numbering (information relating to other volumes in this set).

Step 32: Previously published edition of this work. Please provide titles and ISBNs.

(Other Formats)

Step 33: Format 2 e.g. eBook.

Step 34: Enter ISBN.

Step 35: Enter retail price.

Step 36: System requirements e.g. Kindle.

Step 37: Format 3, e.g. eBook.

Step 38: Enter ISBN.

Step 39: Retail price.

Step 40: System Requirements, e.g. ePub.

Step 41: Comments. Enter any comments or extra information.

Step 42: How would you like us to send the CIP entry?

Step 43: Attached files, if any (optional).

Step 44: Click on 'Submit' button.

Please note that after pressing the 'Submit' button a confirmation page will be displayed and attachments can be uploaded at this point. Once the application is submitted, a confirmation page will appear, which should have an application number e.g. NLApp45699. A confirmation email will also be sent to the publisher contact email entered in the application form.

For your free checklist, go to
www.dyanburgess.com/resources

NOTES:

Will I complete the Cataloguing-in-Publication submission?

Do I have all the information that I need to complete the submission?

Will someone help me?

Where will I find someone to help me?

What tools can I use from the tools list?

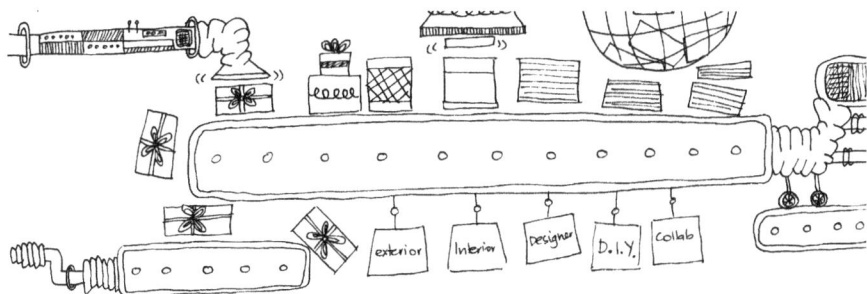

Step

4

BAKE YOUR BOOK
(BOOK DESIGN—INTERIOR)

THE RIGHT DESIGN FOR YOUR BOOK

When baking a cake, you make something you know the people who will be eating it are going to like. It's the same with a book; you need to think about your audience. Choosing the design of your cake needs to resonate with the message you want to deliver and the reason you are celebrating. Similarly, your book will send your message based on its design.

As the book publishing industry knows, many people do judge a book by its cover.

As with baking a cake, you will have a budget. As many a great cook knows, keeping it simple is the key to any recipe. The same rule applies to publishing.

The following two sections, 'Bake Your Book' and 'Continue Baking Your Book', are about the design of your book, inside and out. I have separated the interior and exterior design to simplify the nuances between the two.

Tools

    a. Upwork (formerly Elance)
    b. Writers' centre in your state
    c. Business associates
    d. Amazon help forums
    e. Google
    f. 99 Designs
    g. Fiverr
    h. You
    i. Independent publishing house (they will do all the running around and you simply oversee)

Whichever order you do your cover and interior design in is your choice. This is another mechanical step. The level of involvement you choose will, again, depend on your interest levels, available time, and money. Things to consider when choosing a designer:

1. See samples of their work.
2. Look at other books that you like elements of, for example: design, colour palettes, or the font you would like to see in your book. I am not suggesting plagiarism or breaching copyright. Some people have difficulty providing verbal or written instruction about what they see in their heads. Using other examples can assist in developing your approach. Just like using Pinterest to inspire ideas about how you would design a cake, similarly save images that will help you design your book, inside and out.
3. There are generally two formats of books.
    a. Paperback. This can also include hardcover.
    b. EBook. This can be any electronic format for, e.g., Kindle books (mobi), Kobo (ePub), other eReaders (again ePub) and PDFs.
4. Some designers can design both formats; some only do one. Again, if this feels too complicated, invest time in talking to publishing houses. They are worth their weight in gold when they align with your wants.

Choosing your designer can seem daunting at first. Having a pre-determined budget will assist your decision-making; it will also mean that you may need to refine some of your ideas for the interior layout.

There are many very talented designers in the marketplace. You may be lucky enough to stumble across the next Chip Kidd (Google him, he is amazing). Simple is best.

With the thought of competing with larger publishing houses, you can feel quite pressured into having the next amazing book design. This book is not about competing with the big publishers in a game they wrote the rules for! Remember, this book is about keeping the steps simple to share your story with the world.

The first version of your story will be the first 'published' iteration. It could be a little rough and a little 'oops, I missed that'. Keep going, this is the key. Ship at every step.

Be proud of what you are doing and how you do it, within your financial capacity and time availability. This pride will shine more than an expensive bill from a designer who makes your book look like it was published by a major publishing house, but has significantly delayed your publication and caused significant costs in the interim.

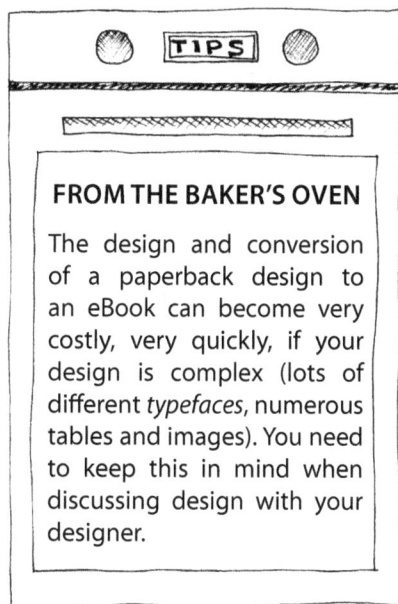

TIPS

FROM THE BAKER'S OVEN

The design and conversion of a paperback design to an eBook can become very costly, very quickly, if your design is complex (lots of different *typefaces*, numerous tables and images). You need to keep this in mind when discussing design with your designer.

Method

The checklist for these steps is in Appendix I.

Following are suggested steps for obtaining quotes and choosing a designer. The aim is find a designer you can work with, at a price you choose to afford, for the outcome you want to achieve. You may want to produce only a paperback, if so ignore the eBook references. Alternatively, if you want to generate an eBook ignore the paperback references. This is your book to choose how you want to publish and present to your audience.

1. Submit manuscript to book designer for quoting on manuscript to be provided in the following formats:
   a. CreateSpace—PDF
   b. Amazon KDP—mobi
   c. Smashwords/other eBooks—ePub
2. Book designer to provide a sample chapter to confirm format.
3. Accept/reject layout from book designer.
4. Book designer then to work on entire book (note—you need to ensure sample provided is included in the full version).
5. Interior files to comply to requirements listed below:
   a. CreateSpace
      i. Black and white book MUST be in black and white in *CMYK* (Cyan, Magenta, Yellow Key) black colour process
      ii. Colour book must be in *CMYK* colour process
      iii. Must be in PDF
   b. Kindle
      i. Mobi format for Amazon Kindle
      ii. Must meet Kindle guidelines
   c. Smashwords/ePub
      i. ePub or MS Word file for Smashwords
      ii. Must meet Smashwords/eBook guidelines
6. Review/approve/decline
7. Confirm final layout

8. Review/approve utilising the review checklist in Appendix J – Proofing Checklist for Printing
9. Save final version with the wording 'FINAL' in the file name. This file will be used to upload to your chosen platforms and will be referred to as the *book interior*.

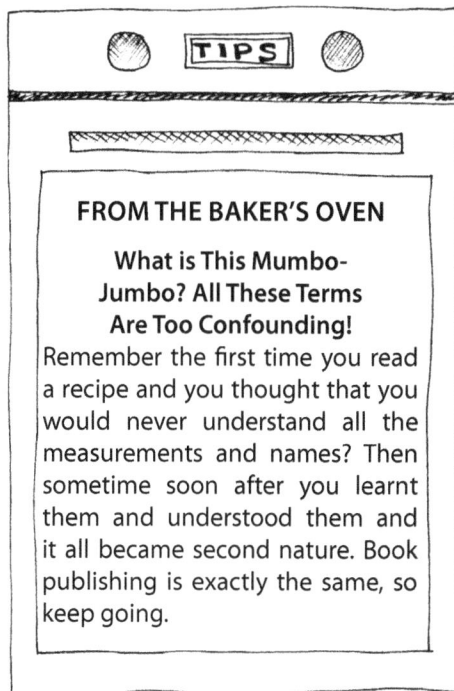

TIPS

FROM THE BAKER'S OVEN

What is This Mumbo-Jumbo? All These Terms Are Too Confounding!

Remember the first time you read a recipe and you thought that you would never understand all the measurements and names? Then sometime soon after you learnt them and understood them and it all became second nature. Book publishing is exactly the same, so keep going.

Becoming an independently published author seems daunting at first. The best thing to remember is that the vast majority of people you meet in the industry want to help you. Take your time to listen and learn. Ask questions when people use industry terms you don't understand.

Also, a great relationship with your designer will ensure you are not lost in this process. They will take care of all these issues for you.

The wording I have used in the checklists is based on the wording provided by the particular distribution platforms.

I reiterate this is about steps for you to follow to increase your chance of success when baking a book. Providing you with an understanding of the processes increases your chances of success. If it seems too much, call in outside help; remember the tools list at the beginning of each step. If these tools are outside your budget, research how to do it yourself. No excuses!

<u>Note:</u> Uploading of the book will be covered in Step 6.

For your free template letters and checklist, go to www.dyanburgess.com/resources

NOTES:

Search for a designer?

Will I use someone from the tools lists?

What costs can I afford?

Is this too much? Money? Time?

Should I use an independent publishing house? What are the costs? What value will they create?

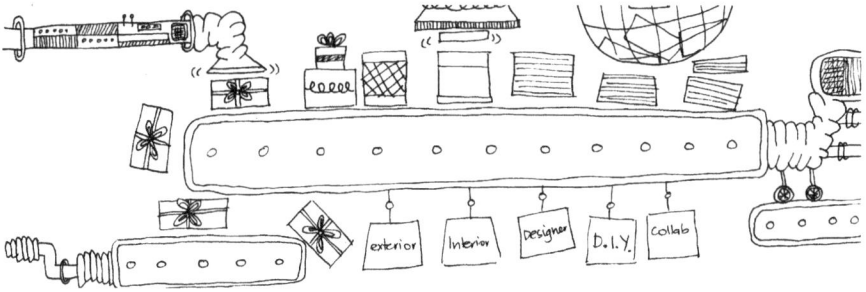

Step

5

CONTINUE
BAKING YOUR BOOK
(BOOK DESIGN—EXTERIOR)

GRAPHIC DESIGN OF YOUR COVER

At this stage, you are wrapping up the final bits and pieces in order for your book to be ready for production; that is, finalising your book for publication. If you have not arranged or designed your cover, now is the time to do it. The tools at this step are the same as for Step 4, which are listed below for easy referencing:

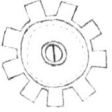

Tools

a. Upwork (formerly Elance)
b. Writers' centre in your state
c. Business associates
d. Amazon help forums
e. Google
f. 99 Designs
g. Fiverr
h. You
i. Independent publishing house (they will do all the running around and you simply oversee)

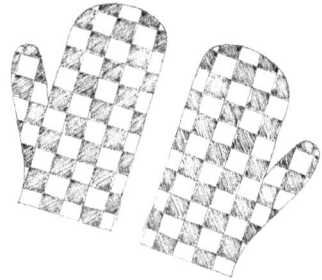

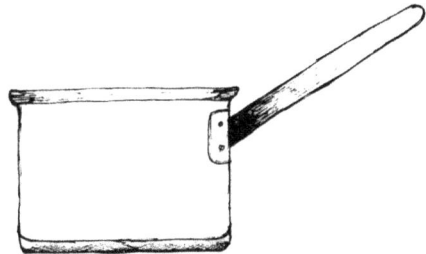

To further elaborate on the cover design, the following table summarises the three alternatives.

D.I.Y.	Collaborative	No Input
1. Design book cover. This could be drawn on an App or other electronic means or on a piece of paper. As long as you are able to email it to the designer that is the main point. Then they can mock up the design ensuring the cover will comply with the requirements of the platform you choose.	Same as D.I.Y. Add in that you would ask the designer for variations to your idea. It is a good idea for the designer to read the manuscript as well.	Provide the designer the manuscript for them to come up with a design.
2. Review design. If okay, then use precedent email to find a designer to action on Upwork (formerly Elance) or Fiverr in Appendix K.		

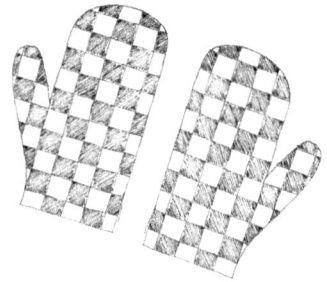

Depending on the graphic designer you choose for your interior, the cover may be part of the arrangement. I have had a spectrum of experiences. Below are samples:

D.I.Y	Collaborative	No input
I drew this up on Paper 53 (App for smartphone and tablets) one afternoon and sent it off to a designer to put it into the correct format for publishing.	Worked with designer by providing a couple of sketched notes. The designer took it from there.	Asked the designer to provide an example. This is the result.

Book Exterior Pre-Publication Checklist

The checklist for these steps is in Appendix L

1. If you want to self-design the book cover, minimum requirements are listed below:
   a. CreateSpace
      i. Cover Must be in *CMYK* colour process
      ii. Must be in *PDF* format with properly formatted for particular printers

      iii. Check *CreateSpace* guidelines
  b. Amazon KDP
      i.   Cover Must be in *RGB* (Red, Green, Blue) colour process
      ii. Cover should be formatted to 1563 x 2500px (*pixels*)
  c. Smashwords/eBook
      i.   Cover must be in *RGB* colour process
      ii. Cover should be formatted to 1600 x 2400px

2. Spine will need to be corrected based on interior file final width; this is why the cover needs to be finalised after the interior is confirmed.

3. No price point on cover. (This is my personal preference, particularly when working in multiple currencies and on multiple platforms. Having a price on your cover can be confusing for the consumer).

4. Request a 3D (three-dimensional) image of the book cover for promotional use while books are in production (these look fantastic).

5. Review/approve and check if there is any formatting to be fixed here.

6. Once proof is okay, save final version with the wording 'FINAL' in the file name. This is file the *book exterior* to be uploaded with your *book interior* to your chosen platforms.

For your free template letters and checklist, go to www.dyanburgess.com/resources

NOTES:

Will I design my cover?

Will I have someone else help me?

What is my budget?

What is my pain threshold? (In other words, when do these processes start to give you stress? This is your pain threshold. It means you need to pass this part of the process to someone else, otherwise you will not finish your book.)

What is my Plan B if I do not ship within the timeframe set?

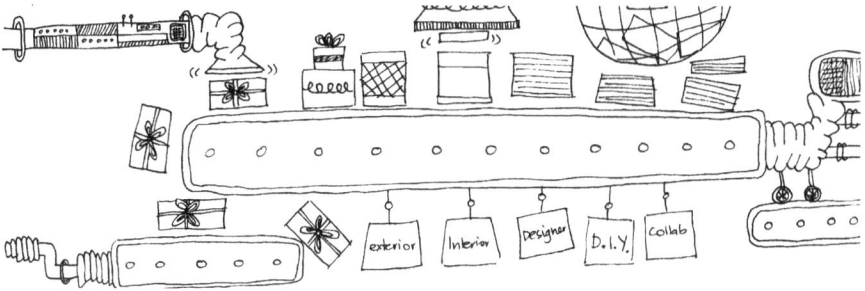

Step 6

CUTTING YOUR CAKE & SHARING IT AROUND (UPLOADING YOUR BOOK TO DISTRIBUTION PLATFORMS)

WHAT PLATFORM(S) SHOULD I USE TO SHARE MY BOOK?

You have baked your cake and created the decorations in line with the message you want to deliver. Now you need to be able share the cake with those who would like to enjoy it.

Similarly, in book publishing you need to decide how and where you will share your book. That is, you will need to decide which platform or platforms you would like to use to distribute your book. If you don't want to be involved in the mechanics, collaborate with an independent publishing house. As mentioned in Step 3, it is about understanding the consequences of your choices, particularly with reference to your available time and finances. If you choose to do these steps yourself, please keep reading.

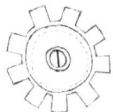

Tools

a. Upwork (formerly Elance)—where you can find talent directly
b. Writers' centre in your state (great free resources)
c. Business associates
d. Amazon help forums
e. Google
f. Independent publishing house

Method

The checklist for these steps is in Appendix M.

a. Upload completed book
   i. CreateSpace (and Lightning Source)

        ◈ Complete info such as book category, price, volume number, publishing date, etc.

   ii. Amazon KDP (Kindle Direct Publishing)

        ◈ Must meet Kindle guidelines.

        ◈ Complete info such as book category, price, volume number, publishing date, etc.

   iii. Smashwords

        ◈ Complete info such as book category, price, volume number, publishing date, etc.

        ◈ Review/approve.

b. Record details of links so you can use on your website and other social media.

c. Update *Author Page* each time a new book or edition is published.

d. Order copies from CreateSpace/Printer.

e. Track book order.

f. Final versions of interior/exterior design to be stored on hard drive and backed up to cloud or back up hard drive.

Each platform has its own rules and regulations about what you can and cannot do, and how to do it. Personally, I use *Amazon's CreateSpace* and *Kindle* platforms, as well as *Smashwords*, *Lightning Source*, local printers, and my own websites. My personal preferences may not be your own. The processes for each platform are similar. You will need to meet the requirements of the platform you choose.
You need to choose and ship.

FROM THE BAKER'S OVEN

Start with one platform, and gain some confidence, then build into the other platforms (ensure you are not breaching any of the legal bits). As an example, Kindle Direct Publishing (KDP) has an exclusive eBook distribution platform for a certain period of time. During that time you cannot sell your eBook anywhere else, including through your own site. Once the exclusive period finishes you can change your arrangements.

For your free checklist, go to www.dyanburgess.com/resources

NOTES:

What platform will I use?

Do I have the expertise or time to do this myself?

Should I bring in someone else to help me?

Who can do this? An independent publishing house? Freelancer?

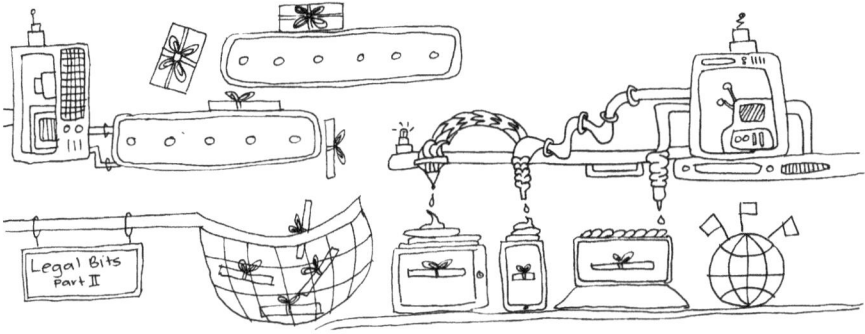

Legal Bits
Part II

Step 7

A BIT MORE LEGAL STUFF (LEGAL DEPOSIT AND ISBN UPDATES)

MORE LEGAL BITS

As with baking a cake you need to clean up after cooking. Tidying up the kitchen after all the work that has been done ensures there is room for more cooking on another day.

Similarly with publishing, you need to tidy up the loose ends of the book publication.

If you don't want to be involved in the mechanics, find a publishing house or a freelancer (check that tools list again) to assist. If you want to be the administrator, read on.

In Australia, it is a legal requirement to lodge both your paperback and eBook (if you publish in this format) for a 'legal deposit' within a particular timeframe of publishing.

Depending on your choice of publication, paperback or eBook, the methods will be slightly different. Ultimately, the result is that you need to provide the deposits—that is, post a hardcopy of your finished paperback, or upload an electronic file of your eBook to the relevant state and national libraries.

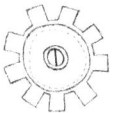

Tools

Again we are looking at tools that were referenced in Step 3.

    a. Upwork (formerly Elance)
    b. Writers' centre
    c. Business associates
    d. Amazon help forums
    e. Google

Method

The checklist for these steps is in Appendix N.

a. Copy or move a final version of the book interior and exterior to *DropBox* (or other back-up platform). I save my final copies in a number of places, including *DropBox*, *Basecamp* and onto a hard drive. In *Basecamp* I set up a new folder with the final files for easier referencing and to reduce the likelihood of uploading a previous version (Yes, I have learnt the hard way with this.) While reloading files is relatively easy, it is time-consuming and not good for your sanity.

b. ISBN input via *My Identifiers*

c. EBook legal deposit http://bishop.slq.qld.gov.au/deposit/external/fastTrack.do?operation=fast&admin_unit=QDL01&workflow=Legal%20deposit-Monographs

d. Legal deposit with your State Library—refer to Appendix O.

e. Legal deposit with the National Library of Australia—refer to Appendix P.

f. Lodge book for *Copyright* (this is not a legal requirement, however highly recommended). http://www.copyright-australia.com/

The following is a summary of the requirement for legal deposits, current as at 2015. Please refer to the National Library of Australia website for the latest rules and regulations.

Legal Deposit Requirements Australia-Wide

Below are extracts from the Legal Deposit website. It is best to review the site at https://www.nla.gov.au/legal-deposit/requirements-australia-wide for the current version of requirements. According to their website:

> Legal deposit is a requirement under the Copyright Act 1968 for publishers and self-publishing authors to deposit a copy of any print work published in Australia with the National Library and, when applicable, the deposit libraries in your home state. Legal Deposit ensures that Australian publications are preserved for use now and in the future.
>
> In addition to depositing with the national library, there are similar requirements for each state and territory. These requirements are listed on the national library's website at https://www.nla.gov.au/legal-deposit/requirements-australia-wide.

An example of eDeposit requirement for Queensland is outlined below. Each Australian state and territory is broadly similar.

FROM THE BAKER'S OVEN

The eDeposit Submission Sample and Template checklist at Appendices Q and R provide a sample of the information that you need to collect to prepare for your submission and a template checklist for you to complete your information relevant to your *title*.

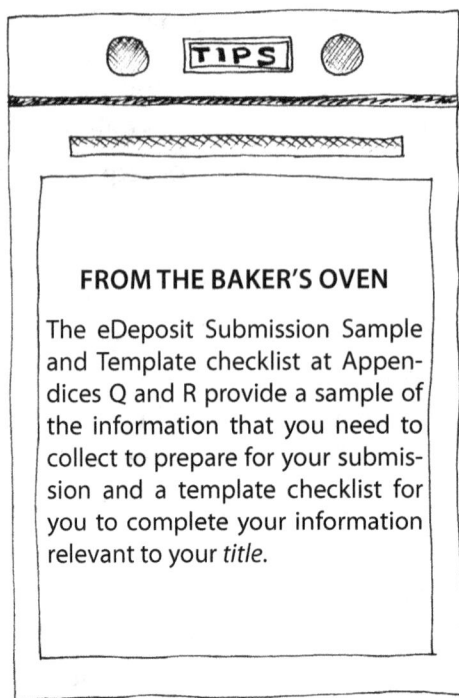

How to Deposit Your Digital Files to the State Library of Queensland

Details for the steps are outlined below. eDeposit-in-Publication is a free service, no registration or login is required. As the eDeposit site notes, this is a step-by-step process that lets you deposit:

- New e-serial titles, such as newsletters, magazines, and journals
- Ongoing serial issues (using a simplified form)
- eBooks, reports, and other monographic resources

Following is a sample of the steps to submit for eDeposit to provide you with a general guide as to the process and what it involves. Then you can decide if you want to be involved or if you want to call in some help.

Step 1: Visit the website: http://bishop.slq.qld.gov.au/deposit/external/ fastTrack.do?operation=fast&admin_ unit=QDL01&workflow=Legal%20 deposit-Monographs

Step 2: Enter the contact name

Step 3: Enter email

Step 4: Enter phone number

Step 5: Enter institute, e.g. D&M Smith Pty Ltd

Step 6: Click 'Next'

Step 7: Choose type of object to be submitted ('Legal Deposit Monographs' is automatically selected by default)

Step 8: Click 'Next'

Step 9: Enter title of the book

Step 10: Year of publication

Step 11: Place of publication, e.g. Queensland

Step 12: Publisher, e.g. D&M Smith Pty Ltd

Step 13: Organisation name, e.g. N/A—if it is published by or on behalf of an agency, department association, or other organisation, complete the organisation name field.

Step 14: Author—if an individual has published it, complete this field.

Step 15: Description (use the blurb on the back of the cover).

Step 16: Keyword (Use words from the description)

Step 17: Web address, e.g. http://www.yourwebsite.com.au/— if this book is available online, enter the web address.

Step 18: Your name. Enter your name as the depositor of this book for contact purposes only. This information is not displayed to the public.

Step 19: Your email

Step 20: Your contact details

Step 21: Access rights—select open access or restricted access. Definition of access rights from the eDeposit registry is as follows: "Open Access: This is the default option for access rights as the state library is committed to providing the widest possible access to electronic legal deposit publications through unrestricted online access via 'One Search'. Restricted Access: If you believe your publication should not be made available online to the general public without restriction, select this option. This is generally applied to commercially available resources. State Library will restrict online use to within State Library's building, thereby providing the same level of access as a print publication."

Step 22: Click 'Next'

Step 23: Copyright statement. Definition of this statement form the eDeposit Registry is as follows: "By submitting the deposited item to the institutional repository you warrant that: The information you provided above is full and correct and that you are either the copyright holder of the deposited item or you are authorized by the copyright holder to submit the item to the Institutional Repository. The deposited material doesn't violate any copyright law. By submitting the deposited item to the Institutional Repository you also agree to provide the Institutional Repository with perpetual, non-exclusive, non-transferable right to take the necessary preservation actions to keep the deposited item accessible, including but not limited to conversion of the deposited material to other formats and making copies of the deposited material."

Step 24: Select 'I accept the terms and conditions'

Step 25: Click 'Next'

Step 26: Upload the file (accepts only PDF format for file type and must be under 25MB)

Step 27: Label the file

Step 28: Click 'Next'

Step 29: Notes: optional

Step 30: Review and confirm information

Step 31: Click 'Submit'

Note: Deposited items will need to be checked by the State Library before they will appear in that library's catalogue.

For your free checklist, go to
www.dyanburgess.com/resources

NOTES:

Will I complete the Legal Deposit myself?

Will someone else assist me?

Which libraries do I need to send my Legal Deposit to? What state or territory, am I based in and what country am I in? Does my book require deposit with the parliamentary library?

What tools should I use from the tools list?

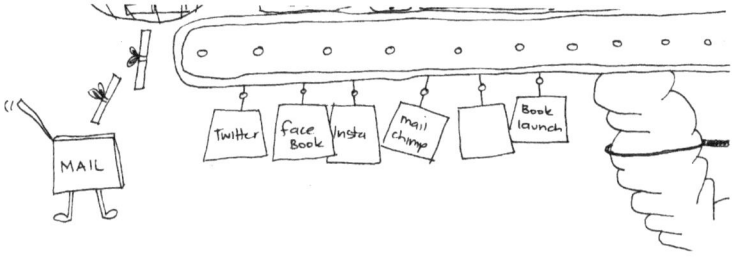

Step

8

FINISHING UP
(MARKETING)

NOW IT IS TIME TO CELEBRATE (AND, WHEN THE REAL WORK STARTS)—YOUR STORY IS SHARED WITH THE WORLD

You have prepared, planned, and crossed off your checklists. How will you market and celebrate your book?

What? Market my book?

A book launch—with a celebratory cake perhaps, in the shape of a book? Sounds delicious!

For those interested in a formal campaign, you know who you are and you probably already have a list of connections to spread the word. For those of you who don't, some options are listed below.

Book marketing is another book in itself. The following tips are starting points for high level planning. Marketing needs to fit with what you are comfortable with and what you have the capacity to commit to. How you choose to celebrate and market your finished book is your choice.

Know that you have been on a journey that many start, but never complete. So again, the key at this step is to ship.

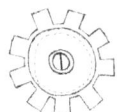 **Tools**

You should be familiar with the first item in the tool list, as it has commenced most of the tools lists for the previous steps, but the others may not be terms or sites you are aware of. Google is your best source to understand the other platforms listed that you are not aware of.

> a. Upwork (formerly Elance)
> b. MailChimp
> c. Buffer
> d. Adwords

e. PR specialist

f. Again, a publishing house can direct you further

Method

The checklist for these steps is in Appendix S.

a. Draft updates for social media websites
- Twitter
- Blog
- MailChimp

b. Review/approve

c. Book to be sent to website content manager
- Front cover only in JPEG (300 dpi)
- Full PDF of book

d. Website Content Manager to arrange book covers, to be uploaded to website with links to:
- CreateSpace
- Amazon KDP
- Smashwords

e. Website Content Manager to arrange:
- Free PDF download hidden page on your website

f. Upload order forms

g. Consider 'Sales Day' (e.g. all books 50% off).

For your free checklist, go to
www.dyanburgess.com/resources

I would love to hear from you and how you are tracking with your story. Please email me at dyan@dyanburgess.com.

For more hints and tips, my blog is at dyanburgess.com/blog, or join my monthly newsletter that I write with Words from Daddy's Mouth with more tips, tricks and interviews with people in the Independent Publishing industry.

NOTES:

How will I market my book?

What platforms do I use already?

LinkedIn

Facebook

Website

Local library

AdWords

URL tracking

Subscribers

Tumblr

Twitter

TV

Radio

Newspapers

Forums

You Did It!

You struggled, you triumphed, and you (hopefully) had some fun along the way. Now you and your story can be read and remembered, shared, and loved. Thank you for sharing your story with the rest of the world, or, at least, with your part of the universe.

Glossary

The terms below will assist you with providing your designer or anyone else who is assisting you, with independent book publishing industry language to allow clearer communication of your thoughts and ideas.

When you see books that you love the look and feel of, take note of what experience you loved about the book. Would you like readers of your book to have the same experience? This will assist when creating your book.

Please note, not all terms in the glossary are used in this book.

Term	Definition
Amazon	As at 2015, Amazon is the largest American-based online retailer. It was established by Jeff Bezos, which started selling books and then diversified its products to include electronics, fashion, video games, software, etc. Kindle Books is the proprietary eBook invented by Amazon and requires a Kindle eReader or the Kindle App to enable reading of the eBooks.
App	Short for the word 'Application' when referring to the program that you download to your smartphone or tablet.
Author Bio/ Page (within a book and online)	In a book this is the page that identifies the author and provides biographical data about them. It may contain their photo. Online platforms such as Amazon, Smashwords, and independent publishing houses have established dedicated author pages, which allow the author to display details about themselves and their publications, as well as an image.

Term	Definition
Barcode	Originally utilised by railway companies to track their equipment, the humble barcode revolutionised the ability of the grocery industry to be able to quickly and easily mark stock and track inventory. The ability to scan a barcode with an optical machine quickly saw the barcode transferred across many industries, including book publishing, to automate tracking, pricing, and updating data of stock.
Basecamp	Basecamp is a cloud-based project management software system. It allows users to monitor and collaborate on a project from end-to-end, you can also add in third parties with limited access, which means you don't need to follow up lots of messy email threads. As an author this can make life so much easier and less confusing for all involved. The other benefit is being able to communicate with each other in real time no matter where the team is based in the world.
Blog	Originally known as a 'weblog', blogging quickly became a platform for people to voice their thoughts in an open forum. Blogs are now an integral part of many businesses' communication with their customer base. Blogs have also created their own 'blogosphere' and there are numerous blog types, from personal, to genre and media, to device-based. Entries on a blog are known as 'posts' and are typically displayed in reverse chronological order (that is, the most recent post is first). As an author a blog can create a community of followers who want to communicate directly with you.
Blurb	The limited text that is on the back cover of a book. Also considered a promotional or publicity statement. It can assist you to clarify your pitch and why you are writing this book at this time.
Book exterior	Simply the outside of the book. In publishing industry terms, the exterior will also be defined by terms such as: hardcover, paperback, and softcover. The type of cover that you choose will depend on the message you want to send to the audience, and your budget.
Book interior	The inside of a book. All those pages that you have been agonising over for months or years, bound together in a logical order for you to share.

Term	Definition
CIP	Cataloguing-in-Publication (CiP) is a free service offered by the National Library of Australia. Essentially it allows your book to be found by libraries on their database as well as extending your listing in their 'Trove' records, which is a catalogue released to a worldwide audience.
Cloud	Cloud is a term that has become common parlance in today's computing world. Essentially, it means that you can access your data no matter what device you are on, no matter where you are in the world. Why, you may ask, would you want to do this? For me, cloud-based programs have allowed me to connect with people all over the world and allow people to run their work schedule within their lives rather than having their work schedule run their lives. A bit extreme? I don't think so. Think of the applications that you use on a daily basis that are cloud-based: iTunes, Spotify, YouTube, Facebook, Instagram, Twitter. All of these applications offer you an 'interface' to log into your account from any device and communicate with a group of people, or the world. You may also be using cloud-based products for your email, balancing your end of financial year accounts, and interacting with your bank. For me, another major benefit is that I know that this offers a back-up to my desktop computer and my back-up hard drive. As an author, knowing that you have another copy of your manuscript if all else has failed is a huge plus.
CMYK	Cyan—Magenta—Yellow—Key. How many times have you changed ink in your printer and not thought twice about what those letters mean? Printing is typically done in this key. Why is this important? What you see on your screen and what comes out of the printer can be different. Your computer screen operates in RGB (Red—Green—Blue) while your printer usually works with CMYK. If illustrations and images are not part of your work then this is not a concern. If you have images then you will want to check how these look printed as compared to your screen and ask for assistance if there is a variation of colour that distracts from your message. When uploading a book to a platform, it will advise what colour key you need to upload your file in. You must follow the requirement, otherwise your book will be rejected. Even if the file is black and white there can be a requirement to provide the file in CMYK black format.

Term	Definition
Copyright	There are different laws for different countries. In Australia copyright refers to the author's legal right to their work, as recognised and protected by law, protecting it from plagiarism, misuse, and false or wrong attribution. You can submit your works as they are completed to the Copyright Agency of Australia. If your work is used in particular environments, for example pages copied for research in a school or university, you will be paid funds for the use of your works.
CreateSpace	Part of the Amazon Group. This platform allows authors to independently publish their work. With help in all aspects of the book creation process from concept to writing and editing, and then supported by marketing and distribution. CreateSpace is a great resource to meet and find marketing strategists, third party editors, illustrators, artists, and other collaborators who can help you develop and launch your work.
Dashboard	This term has become commonly used with businesses realising that they need a user-friendly interface (web page) that allows users to easily navigate through all the data input and information required. It has been suggested that it is similar to an automobile dashboard because of the way they can be used as a guidance system to get you where you need to go, in a virtual sense.
Database/s	A collection of data that is easily accessed and managed because of its organisation and structure. In the world of 'internet this and cloud that', it is inevitable that you will be part of a database for something, somewhere. As an author you will become part of the database of the platform you choose to use; for example, Amazon, or part of the National Library Archive Database.
Digital Printing	The evolution of digital printing has become the cornerstone for short run printing to be available at a relatively low cost for the independent author. While the quality of digital printing may not be as high as the *offset printing* technique, allowing authors to reduce their costs for production and the risk of holding large volumes of stock is, almost always, worth the trade-off. Should you have large success with your publication you can look at the more expensive large print run options. However, until then, the digital print option will be your best friend.

Term	Definition
Dropbox	This is a cloud-based file-hosting service that allows data storage, cloud access, and user interface, all combining to make possible the storage, dissemination, and sharing of huge amounts of data that would have been difficult to send or transfer through normal email channels. Users are given their own individual folders to access their stored data in the cloud through many channels such as laptops, desktops, tablets, and mobile phones. As an author the ability to know that your manuscript and research is stored somewhere other than on your computer is a relief. This also means that it is easier to share with others who will collaborate with you on your book.
eBook	Electronic book or a publication in digital form, which is usually read online or downloaded onto an eReader device.
eReader	The collective name for devices such as Kindle, Kobo, and Nook, which are specific electronic readers for eBooks that allow the user to store multiple books for reading on the device. (The range of books able to be stored varies from reader to reader, however is generally between 2000 to 3500 books). EReaders were developed to move away from the backlit experience of reading on a computer or mobile screen that can cause eyestrain with the light directed into your eye. The eReader uses e-ink, which is intended to mimic a paperback experience and cause less eyestrain. I constantly have conversations with people about the use of the eReader compared to paperback. For me you can't beat the convenience of the eReader for travel and portability. I can have 5 books on the go and not worry about what page I was on and where I left my books, and my eReader (Kindle) syncs back to my smartphone (iPhone) and tablet (iPad). I have a wish list of apps on the go and one of them is that an app developer makes an app that allows me to be able to handwrite on my eBooks, draw pictures, post sticky notes, and highlight sections, like I do with my paperbacks, and have those notations sync across all my devices … ok I have said it, now let's see how long until the universe sorts it out for me. Evernote and OneNote have similar ideas working in their platforms, however they're not quite the vision that I see.

Term	Definition
End papers	End and front papers are only produced with hardcover books. The method of constructing hardcover books requires 'end papers' to attach the interior neatly to the exterior. End papers can be one piece of coloured paper; or illustrated/images. Changing printing techniques and technology are making this method available to soft cover books as well. Having images or text on the end papers can be a great design enhancement for your book.
ePub	This is the standard file format for International Digital Publishing Forum. Essentially, there are two types of eBooks: mobi, which is exclusive to Amazon, and ePub, which is used by everyone else. Feels a little VHS and Beta (for those who remember that race!).
Fishpond.com	Originally established by Daniel Robertson in 2004 as the first online bookstore in New Zealand. With a slogan of 'millions of books, music and movies' it has a firm following with sales in 2013 of 20,000 per day.
Font	During the time of analogue printing the definition of font was important as it let the typesetter know what point size and typeface they needed to select when putting together the letters into a frame. With the rise of computers, font became interchanged with typeface. As you will see when you use the font menu in Microsoft Word, it asks which font you would like to use, not which typeface. Technically, font is a subset of a typeface, however the digitisation of typesetting has changed the use of these words.
Format	This term in publishing can relate to a number of meanings. Typesetting, formatted text, layout of the book or simply the type of book. The context of the use of the word should assist with which meaning is being referred to. For example, 'the format of the book will be 6 by 9 inches with approximately 200 pages'. Here format relates to what the size and look of book will be once printed. Another example is the format of the book is to be based on large areas of white space.
Front Papers	Refer to 'End papers' above.

Term	Definition
Gloss	This refers to the finish of the paper (interior) or cardboard (exterior). If it is shiny then it is likely to have a gloss finish. The treatment to obtain a gloss finish is different for paper (interior) and cardboard (exterior). A book exterior will need to be treated with a gloss cellulose cover to allow this finish. The 'gloss vs matte' finish is a personal consideration, depending on the market that you are appealing to, the content of your book and your budget.
Google	It is hard not to know about this word in today's internet-based world. According to Wikipedia, Google was a mis-spell of the word 'googol', which is the name for the number one followed by one hundred zeros. Regardless, the name is now part of many people's vocabulary, with 'Google it' being the answer for many questions raised by people young and old. The ability to have a search engine (technical name for the program that searches for the answer to your words in your search function) operate with such a broad scope has allowed consumers to find and relate to products and people in a way that had not been previously possible. While Google lives by the mantra 'do no evil' the information that is available to the 'Googleverse' remains controversial. Each time you log onto your computer and are connected to the internet Google is watching what you do. (Fox Mulder would be saying, "The truth is out there.") The point here is to learn how this can work for you as an author and how to expand your audience with consistent messages wherever you mark your thoughts on the internet.
GSM	This is initialism for 'Grams per Square Metre'. GSM refers to paperweight. As a point of reference standard photocopying paper is usually 80gsm. Unfortunately not all papers are made the same and while 80gsm may be the paperweight that you are advised to use it is good to ask for a sample so that you can see what it looks and feels like before you confirm if you will use it.
Hardback/ hardcover	A book with a cover that is made of cardboard, leather, or cloth, in other words the book cover, feels hard and is inflexible.
Hardcopy	A term like 'hardcopy' has evolved with the internet and computers. Hardcopy is the printed-paper version of a document, book, or publication, as compared with its digital counterpart, which is called a softcopy.

Term	Definition
Hyperlink	When hovering your mouse over a document or an internet page you will notice the ability to 'click' on certain underlined contents. This is called a hyperlink. It makes life easier for the user of your book or website to be able to easily reference the data referred to simply by clicking on it. In books, this can also be used to allow readers to 'click' directly to a chapter.
Imprint page	Traditionally this page was found within the first few pages of opening a book. Now with the rise of more input by authors in independent publishing, imprint pages are finding themselves often at the back of a book. Essentially, it is a summary page of the bibliographic information of the book: author details, publisher, and cataloguing details can be found here.
ISBN	Initialism for 'International Book Standard Number'. Essentially the allocation of a number to each book issued under a title. For example, *Bake a (Business) Book* has an ISBN for the paperback version, another ISBN for the Kindle (mobi) version, and another ISBN for the ePub version. These numbers assist with the cataloguing and tracking of all books published on all media types.
JPEG	Initialism for 'Joint Photographic Experts Group' which is known as a process that compresses files with colour images into a fraction of their actual size. File names have the '.jpeg' letters as the extension to identify this file type.
Justification	This is how your text sits on the page as compared to the margins of the page. Let's take a look at this. Here is an example of left justification. You will see that the text lines up with the left hand margin. Here is an example of right justification. You will see that the text lines up with the right hand margin. Here is an example of centre justification. You will see that the text lines up with the centre margin. Here is an example of full justification. You will see that the text usesthefullspaceavailablewithintheleftandrighthandmargins. Your graphic designer will assist with the appropriate justification for your book when you are at the design stage.

Term	Definition
KDP	Initialism for 'Kindle Direct Publishing', which is the Amazon platform to allow independent authors and publishers to upload and publish their books using the Kindle program. There are supporting tools within this platform to assist with all aspects of publication.
Kerning	Refers to the spaces between letters. This is shown as follows: Kerningthatistootight. Kerning that is standard. Wide kerning. The aim is to make reading the text as easy as possible for your audience.
Kindle	This is the device that is required to read Amazon Kindle books. You can also purchase content direct from the Amazon store through the Kindle. EBooks within the Kindle platform are done on the proprietary code, mobi, developed by Amazon. The common code within the publishing industry for writing eBooks is the ePub format. If you want your eBook on Amazon you need to put it in mobi format.
Kobo	eBook reader developed by Toronto-based Kobo Inc.
Legal deposit	By law you are required to send a copy of all forms of published books, printed and electronic versions, to your state/territory and country libraries, and on occasion to your Parliamentary library.
Lower Case	This refers to the 'small' version of letters when typing for example a, b, c, d as compared to A, B, C, D, which are uppercase. The naming of lower case is derived from the days when printing was done letter by letter on a printing press. The smaller letters were stored in the lower part of the case (the shelving system for the hundreds of letters that the typesetter needed easy access to), hence 'lower case'.
Manuscript	Any handwritten or typewritten document. In the days before printers and computers, to produce a manuscript was very time consuming. While developing a manuscript is still an involved process the ability to utilise technology to leverage other medias to create your manuscript makes the process much more accessible to everyone. Say for example, a person who cannot type or write easily, could videotape or dictate their manuscript and be helped to transcribe it into a paper manuscript. The doors that this opens are numerous.

Term	Definition
Matte	Flat finish of paper as compared to gloss, which is shiny. When deciding about the design of your cover you will need to consider what type of finish you would like. Having your collection of ideas about other books that you like will assist with providing your designer and printer clearer guidance on what you see in your mind as the final result.
Metadata	Is simply data. Traditionally metadata was centralised in library catalogues to assist users to find relevant information in relation to their search topic. With the coming of the digital age this has expanded to all digital platforms. Good metadata will assist browsers find relevant information more easily. You can see where Search Engine Optimisation starts to become a part of metadata on the internet.
Mobi	Proprietary file type for Amazon Kindle books, i.e. the eBook file type, which can only be read with Kindle readers or the Kindle app.
Moleskine	Moleskine was developed to bring back the 'little black notebook'. According to Moleskine's website, Bruce Chatwin was the main catalyst in the Moleskine story. He apparently gave the book its name and was known to buy all the Moleskines he could before he travelled. It seems that Bruce was not the only one who loved these notebooks, and the revival of these books in 1997 by a Milanese printer has seen new generations continue their passion of handwriting notes.
Nook	An eReader developed by bookstore Barnes and Noble. There is the Nook device, and the tablet option is the Samsung Galaxy or the Nook app.
Offset printing	A printing process that transfers an inked image from a plate to a rubber blanket and then to the paper. Very commonly used process for printing based on the sharpness of the result. Preference is for use for larger print runs of books as there is a minimum set up time and cost to have printing done using this technique.
Paperback	A book that has a flexible card or stiff paper as its cover. The interior is usually glued (*perfect bound*) together instead of being stitched or stapled. Most books you see in books stores are paperbacks.

Term	Definition
PX pixels	Origin of the word is from the words picture (pix) and element (el), and became pixel. Represented as px, this is the smallest element in a digital image. This drives the resolution of the images that you see in the digital world around you. Are the images you see clear or are the fuzzy? For example on your phone you will usually have a 540 by 960 pixel resolution while your High Definition Television will be in the range of 1080 by 1090 pixels. If you try to watch a video or look at an image that was made for a smartphone on a computer screen the image will look fuzzy and in chunks of squares (you will see those individual pixels).
PDF	Initialism for 'Portable Document Format'. It may be an image, illustration, or the digital equivalent of a printed page or pages that may be viewed, read, shared, and sent electronically.
Perfect bound	Usual process for binding paperback books. The individual pages of a book and its cover are bound together by an adhesive. This is usually done under heat then pressure to stabilise the construction of the book.
Plain text	With the age of word processing, 'code' or 'hidden instructions' are part of documents to allow elements like font type, paragraph spacing, and margins to be transferred from one word processing program to another. This information can sometimes cause issues between word processing programs and email readers. Plain text removes all the 'code' so that only the text remains. While the formatting and pretty type choices won't be able to be displayed with this option at least you can read what is meant to be read.
PNG	Initialism for 'Portable Network Graphics' or the compression of files without loss in data. Finding formats that allow designers to transfer files for use in a reliable way has seen the invention of the png file type.
POD	Initialism for 'Print-on-Demand'. This process has changed the landscape of the publishing industry. The ability to print a few books for relatively little money has opened up opportunities for the independent author. Particularly in a world of 'long tail' demands (Chris Anderson—*Wired*) where consumers want niche products. Print-on-Demand delivers this opportunity to authors and consumers.

Term	Definition
Print run	When you want to order a batch of books in bulk from a publishing house it is known as a print run. Each publishing house will have requirements for a minimum number of books to be printed in a print run. Alternatively, a company like Amazon, which has CreateSpace as its POD division, allows orders of only one book. The quality of the book varies depending on a number of factors and depending on the result that you want to achieve you may need to spend some time researching the type of POD printer that will suit your needs.
Proof	First copy of the book in printed format, although proofs may be produced digitally as well. Never underestimate the value of a proof to review and reconsider your book. It is important to see your work in print before you hit the final print button.
Proofreading	Reading the manuscript to spot errors and implement minor corrections to grammar and punctuation. It is important to understand the differences in the editing process. Each level of editing considers particular components of a manuscript. When working with an editor ask for clarity around what they will actually be doing for you and whether this will get your book to the final version. Terms used by editors can be confusing. Be sure to clarify what you are actually paying for.
Redline	See Track Changes.
Rich text format	Type of document format produced by Microsoft Word and one that is read by many processors.
Saddle stitch	Thread is sewn in sections to tie the pages of the book together.
Sentence case	The capitalisation of the first letter in the first word of a sentence or heading.
SEO	Initialism for 'Search Engine Optimisation'. Optimising your SEO to make you 'number one' in a range of key search words so you can be found at the stroke of a key or two is ubiquitous. This is a double-edged sword for the consumer. Typing in keywords will show you what you have searched, however is it what you want to search for? Integrity and honesty of your data becomes the cornerstone of your messages to the world.
Title case	The capitalisation of the first letter in the relevant words in a sentence. An example is 'The Title of this Book is the Title'.

Term	Definition
Smashwords	An eBook distributor company founded by Mark Coker that assists independent writers and publishers to connect with eBook retailers. Writers have absolute control over their work throughout its various phases, from editing, marketing, and distribution, to sales.
Title	What is the name of your book? This is called the 'title'—more technically, the distinct name of a piece of work, such as a book, a chapter, a song or musical composition, a poem, a portrait, a short story, a novel, or other such material. Being an author, the main use of the word 'title' will be around the wording that is on the front cover of your book. It is important to understand this word as it is used in many cases for data entry and it is important to be consistent with your data entry.
Track Changes	Function in word processing programs that allows users to makes changes and comments to a document in a manner that can immediately be seen by others for easier editing and feedback.
Trim Size	Technical term for the length and breadth of your book. Term comes from 'trimming' the paper to the same standard size.
Typeface	The history of written language is long. Since the beginning of the use of an alphabet, from those first Phoenician scratches to the modern English alphabet, people have defined their artistic nuances of the written language. How we formed the tools used to generate it initially restricted letters. First sticks, stones, and fingers, then brushes and feathers until the print press came along. With the print press came typeface. Typesetters would meticulously set up thousands of letters into cases to create words, sentences, and paragraphs ready for an ink roller to pass over before being transferred to paper. In saying this, print allowed the duplication of information as never before where books needed to be handwritten if a duplicate was to be made. The setting up of the letters in their casings ready for printing became known as the typeface.

Term	Definition
Typeface (continued)	Now with computers it seems that there are no rules to stop a typeface from becoming a reality. As in the old adage however, just because you can, should you? There are some typefaces that should never have seen the light of day, but then again maybe they helped to inspire a typeface that is more readable. A beautiful book titled *What's My Type* by Simon Garfield provides a wonderful history of type and fonts in all their glory and splendour. Reading the history of those type designers cutting individual letters provides a whole new respect for what they did to create the typefaces of their times. They applied such skill and care to make reading a better experience for the general population. So what is a typeface? It is a series of fonts that each have their own unique design. Common typefaces are Times New Roman and Arial. Within these typefaces are the font subsets, for example, 10-point italic would be a font type.
Typeset	The procedure of placing letters into a format that will make it ready for printing. In the days of the print press this was the inserting of thousands of letters into a case; today what you simply have is typed up in Word, or you can arrange for a graphic designer to be involved and make things more fancy.
Typography	One might argue that typography is an art form in itself. The history of typography is tied with the commentary around typeface. Dictionary.com defines it as: Noun: 1. The art or process of printing with type. 2. The work of setting and arranging types and of printing from them. 3. The general character or appearance of printed matter.
Upper case	Often referred to as capital letters. The history of uppercase is related to that of lower case discussed earlier in this glossary. The placement of the letters in the typesetter's shelving system created the name. The capital letters were stored in the upper part of the case (the shelving system for the hundreds of letters that the typesetter needed easy access to), hence 'upper case'.
URL	Initialism for 'Uniform Resource Locator' or the address of a webpage. For example http://www.dyanburgess.com

Term	Definition
Upload	When you send a file (word document, image or video) to a cloud based platform (Facebook, Twitter, Basecamp) you are uploading that file to the platform. The technical definition may be along the lines of the transmission of electronic data from one server to another for the purpose of storing the file so that other parties can access it.
Version Control	Each time you save your manuscript you should label it with details such as the date, book title, and the version number you are up to. For example, when working on *Bake a Business Book* my progressive files looked like this, with the numbers at the start representing the year/month/day (e.g. 28 August 2015): 150828 v8 *Bake a Business Book*.docx 150909 v9 *Bake a Business Book*.docx This allows easy referencing for the date the changes were made and what iteration the book is at.
Wrap text	One of the functions in Word is the ability to 'wrap' text in particular ways with an image. Your options are: In line with text Square Tight Through Top and Bottom None When in the menu, for Microsoft Office Word, you will usually be provided with an image of what each of functions look like. However, if your focus is the writing leave this detail to your graphic designer.
www	Initialism for 'World Wide Web' and is usually found at the beginning of the hyperlink or URL for a page.

Websites	Website links
3e innovative	www.3e.net.au
Amazon	www.amazon.com
Australian Writers Centre	www.writerscentre.com.au
Basecamp	www.basecamp.com
BowkerThorpe	www.bowker.com
CreateSpace	www.createspace.com
Dyan Burgess	www.dyanburgess.com
Editors (The Institute of Professional Editors Limited)	www.iped-editors.org
Upwork (formerly Elance)	www.upwork.com
InHouse Publishing	www.inhousepublishing.com.au
Kindle	www.kindle.amazon.com
Kobo Books	www.store.kobobooks.com/en-US
Lending rights	www.arts.gov.au/literature/lending_rights
National archives	www.naa.gov.au
Nielsen	www.nielsen.com/us/en.html
Nook Books	www.barnesandnoble.com/u/NOOK-Book-eBook-store
Moleskine	www.moleskine.com/au
My Identifiers	www.myidentifiers.com.au
Queensland Writers Centre	www.qwc.asn.au
Smashwords	www.smashwords.com
Text Publishing	www.textpublishing.com.au
Transcription	www.jessetranscriptions.com
Words from Daddy's Mouth	www.wordsfromdaddysmouth.com.au

Appendices

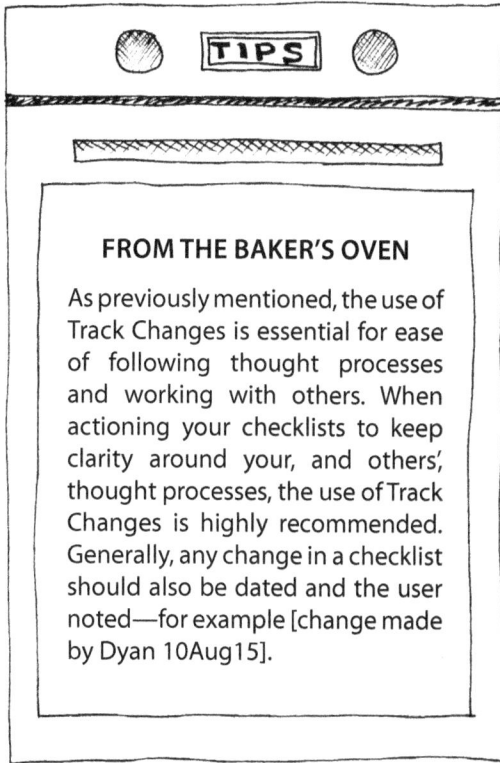

TIPS

FROM THE BAKER'S OVEN

As previously mentioned, the use of Track Changes is essential for ease of following thought processes and working with others. When actioning your checklists to keep clarity around your, and others', thought processes, the use of Track Changes is highly recommended. Generally, any change in a checklist should also be dated and the user noted—for example [change made by Dyan 10Aug15].

APPENDIX

A

QUICK USER GUIDE

CREATING A (BUSINESS) BOOK – QUICK USER GUIDE

Below is a general outline of issues and tasks to consider when creating a book. While there are various types of books, and the specifics may ultimately differ, the issues and tasks below should be considered. It is a good idea to update the table as you go to ensure issues and tasks are not overlooked.

No.	Issues to Consider	Response
1	Open a new folder on your computer, or in Basecamp, and label it '[Your Book Title]'.	
2	Create an internal issues list to centralise additional considerations and source documents used.	
3	Consider the style for the book, e.g. will the book contain chapters or will it be a short book?	
4	Consider the topic for the book and compile relevant articles, fact sheets, and blog posts. Centralising them into a single document in a structured way is usually the best way to do this.	
5	When working up the book, please consider the guidelines or standards for your genre and if they need to be followed. That is, copy and paste the content into the book and rearrange in a structured way. Once arranged, make amendments in Redline so that the changes to the settled source documents can be easily seen.	
6	Ensure paragraphs do not repeat themselves in the book as source content may contain the same paragraph or information.	

No.	Issues to Consider	Response
7	Ensure terms are defined only once. Also, consider whether it is worth defining particular terms.	
8	Consider if footnotes are to be used. If footnotes are not to be used, ensure the information is otherwise integrated into the book.	
9	Consider if a glossary should be used.	
10	Consider if a contents page is appropriate.	
11	Ensure the chapter flows for consistency (style and formatting).	
12	Ensure all wording is 'timeless', if possible—e.g. avoid using terms such as 'recently', 'as discussed above', etc.	
13	If blog posts are used, consider integrating them as case studies or examples.	
14	Ensure all diagram formatting is consistent and is of high quality.	
15	Ensure that there are no annexures or schedules, unless appropriate. These should be integrated into their respective chapters of the book.	
16	Ensure a checklist review is undertaken at least twice, including before submitting to graphic designer.	
17	Include an introductory paragraph and a blurb (that will be inserted on the back cover of the book).	
18	Include additional sections for 'About the team', 'Acknowledgements', and 'Disclaimers' before the 'Introduction'. Ensure you acknowledge all contributing authors by name in the 'Acknowledgements'.	
19	Provide the document to a colleague to review.	
20	Once settled, the author should arrange for the book to be reviewed by a publisher/editor.	
21	Consider using an external copyeditor/proofreader.	

APPENDIX

B

MANUSCRIPT DEVELOPMENT CHECKLIST

MANUSCRIPT DEVELOPMENT CHECKLIST

No.	Summary of issue to be checked	Tick once checked
1	Review your manuscript in the following steps: • Big picture/overall look: Flick through the pages. Does the style flow; are your headers and footers consistent? • Pages: Are pages correctly separated? • Paragraphs: Is the style consistent? How many spaces do you have? • Sentences: Grammar check in Microsoft Word can be a good start. • Words/typos: Again use of Microsoft Word spell check is a good starting point; ensure you choose correct language for English (e.g. UK). • Formatting: Get into the detail here. Have you used the same style bullet points, are your quotes consistently styled? Setting up a checklist or table of your styles/formatting can assist to ensure consistency.	
2	Consistent *typeface* for entire manuscript. Most book designers can adjust if needed. However in my experience there are less likely to be errors or confusion if this is clear from the outset.	
3	Chapters to be *hyperlinked* to contents page (this is optional as some designers prefer to do the contents page links themselves).	

No.	Summary of issue to be checked	Tick once checked
4	Confirm your *author bio* is up to date. When was the last time you checked your details and your picture? Your *author bio* needs to be congruent with who you are and what you look like now, not twenty years ago. Please, no airbrushing. It is very confusing, particularly if you are a public speaker or regularly present to your audience.	
5	*Blurb* (the text on the back cover) is also a great way to refine the pitch of your book. Some would suggest you get this right first. Interestingly, well-known children's author Emma Walton Hamilton, notes the importance of this when marketing your book.	
6	Acknowledgements and thank yous. Work out the list of people who have been there for you and helped you along the way so far. You can always add more names as they arise.	
7	Format to be how you want the final version i.e. new chapter, new page. Again, this assists the editor and designer to understand your thoughts and provides a clear flow of text throughout the book.	
8	Headers on interior pages of book: book title LHS (left hand side) and chapter title RHS (right hand side) this is my personal preference.	
9	Complete all aspects of *Document Review Checklist (Appendix C)*.	
10	Consider further reviews by friends, family, and local and overseas resources.	

APPENDIX

C

CHECKLIST FOR DOCUMENT REVIEW

Before I send a book to an editor I run a basic edit and grammar check. Having a manuscript as tidy as possible before the first run to the editor can save time, money, and confusion for everyone. The checklist following is the one I apply.

No.	Summary of issue to be checked	Tick once checked
1	Author details confirmed against source documentation *Are there additional authors to those listed on the front cover	
2	Document read from last page to first page (in that order)	
3	Spell check	
4	Grammar check	
5	General punctuation	
6	Consistent formatting throughout (including semicolons, colons, quotations, defining terms, etc.) *A subheading is typically written in title case, but this rule can be appropriated as long as it is consistent throughout the document.	
7	Style guide followed correctly	
8	Use of 'find' function on any words replaced in the document	
9	All footers checked for accuracy, including page numbers	
10	Table of contents updated at the end of all amendments	
11	Confirmation that all terms defined in the body of the document or used in title case are listed in the definition section and that terms are only defined once and in the first place they appear	

No.	Summary of issue to be checked	Tick once checked
12	Correct tense used throughout the document and used consistently	
13	All external references checked (for example, footnotes, etc.)	
14	Confirmation that all terms in the definition section are used in the document—must use 'find' function to confirm this	
15	Confirmation that all diagrams in the document are accurate and in high quality format	
	*Provide the graphic designer the diagrams in a PDF to ensure that the integrity of the diagrams is held together	
16	Confirmation that all names are entirely correct wherever used	
17	Confirmation that dates wherever used are correct	
18	Consistent cross referencing throughout the document— manually check this	
19	Use 'find' function on: 1. double full stops (..) 2. double spacing ( ) 3. the word 'error' 4. '#' 5. space comma (,) 6. semicolon comma (;,)	
20	Confirm all author notes have been read and deleted	
21	Ensure that any update to source documentation or precedents is made in real time	
22	Confirm all salutations in the correspondence are correct (for example, if the character is a doctor)	
23	Are all definitions in alphabetical order	
24	Has all meta data been removed	
25	Is the formatting consistent throughout the document	
26	Has a hardcopy of the document been printed and manually reviewed	
27	Ensure a scanned copy of the complete document with all handwritten suggestions and amendments together with the completed checklist are sent back to the relevant person	

APPENDIX

D

EDITING QUOTE CHECKLIST

No.	Summary of issue to be checked	Tick once checked
1	Submit manuscript to editor for them to quote their price.	
2	Editor to provide a sample chapter to confirm style and all changes in *Redline* (also known as *Track Changes*).	
3	Accept/reject editing from editor.	
4	Editor then to work on entire book (need to ensure original sample provided is included into the full version of the final manuscript).	
5	Review/approve/decline *tracked changes*. Ensure date and version number are included on your file name—for example, '150828 v3 Book Title.docx'—where the year, month, and date are the first number of the file name. Allows for easier tracking later.	
6	Provide feedback.	
7	Review/approve.	
8	Save final version with the wording 'FINAL' in the file name. This file is then provided to the book designer.	

APPENDIX

E

ISBN TRACKING LIST

Set up a table in a central location, for example your project management system, or in a folder on your computer. This table will list all your ISBNs, which have and have not been allocated a book title. This can save time and confusion when reconciling with Bowker-Thorpe or if you need to quickly look up which ISBN belongs where.

Date Issued	ISBN	Title	Format Type
	1234567890123	The First Book	ePub
	1234567890124	The First Book	Mobi
	1234567890125	The First Book	Paperback
	1234567890126	The First Book	Hardback
	1234567890127		Unallocated

You will see from this example that one 'title' can have many ISBNs, as each format requires a separate ISBN.

APPENDIX
F
MY IDENTIFIERS CHECKLIST AND INPUT GUIDE

My Identifiers is the data collection program for your ISBNs. This is one of those legal bits that you need to ensure is completed accurately and in a timely manner. This also assists with people being able to search your ISBN and be provided with the correct information.

No.	Title & Cover	Notes
1	Title	
2	Subtitle	
3	Main description	
4	Original publication date	
5	Current language	
6	Translated title	
7	Copyright year	
8	Upload cover image (held in Dropbox ISBN/ cover)	
9	Upload the full text of the book—max size 40MB (held in Dropbox ISBN/PDF content)	
10	Contributors	
11	Contributor's name (it may be a person or entity. You can add as many contributors as needed)	
12	Contributor's first and last name	
13	Contributor function	
14	Contributor biography—350 words max (held in Dropbox ISBN/author bio)	
15	Format and size	
16	Medium	

No.	Title & Cover	Notes
17	Format	
18	Format details	
19	Packaging description	
20	Trade catalogue	
21	Primary subject	
22	Secondary subject	
23	Weight unit	
24	Weight	
25	Number of pages	
26	Number of illustrations	
27	Carton quantity	
28	Size units	
29	Length, width, height	
30	Title volume number	
31	Total volume number	
32	Edition number	
33	Special editions (select from drop-down)	
34	Point size	

APPENDIX
G
CIP SUBMISSION SAMPLE

The following is an example of the information needed to submit your book for Cataloguing-in-Publication. This is a guide to assist you in gathering the correct information and data before you submit to save you time and frustration. You may want to do this yourself or you may want to pass on to someone else to complete.

No.	Description	Information	Notes
1	Publisher Name	D&M Smith	
2	Publisher category	Individual	
3	Address	P.O. Box 1234	
4	City/Town/Suburb	New Place	
5	State	QLD	
6	Postcode	4000	
7	Phone contact	123 456 789	
8	Fax contact	123 459 789	
9	Email address	jo@jones.com	
10	Contact Name	Jo Jones	
11	Book Title	Love at First Sight	
12	Subtitle	How to Recognise It	
13	Edition	1	
14	Imprint	D&M Smith	
15	Format 1	PDF	
16	ISBN—remove dashes	9712312312312	
17	Retail price	$29.95	
18	System requirements (eBook/paperback/ hardback/loose-leaf/cd)	Paperback	
19	Planned year of publication	2015	

No.	Description	Information	Notes
20	Planned month of publication	December	
21	Authors/contributors listed on the title page e.g. John Smith (author)	Jo Jones (author) Book design by Book Design Interior book layout by Sam Smith	
22	Life Dates/middle names of author/contributor	Jo Joe Jones	
23	Description of the book	A collection of stories	
24	Genre of audience—fiction or nonfiction and children/play/poetry/short stories	Nonfiction—Other	
25	Primary audience (general reader, pre-school age, etc.)	General readers	
26	Series title		Leave it blank if it doesn't apply
27	Series numbering		Leave it blank if it doesn't apply
28	Bibliography/index		Leave it blank if it doesn't apply
29	Multivolume numbering (information relating to other volumes in this set)		Leave it blank if it doesn't apply
30	Previously published edition of this work and ISBN		Leave it blank if it doesn't apply
FORMAT 2		**EBOOK**	
1	ISBN—remove dashes	E.g. 9712312312312	
2	Retail price	E.g. $19.95	
3	System requirements (eBook/paperback/hardback/loose leaf/cd)	Kindle	
FORMAT 3			
1	ISBN—remove dashes		
2	Retail price		

No.	Description	Information	Notes
3	System requirements (eBook/paperback/ hardback/loose leaf/cd)		
4	Enter comments (any comments or extra information you'd like to add)		Optional
5	Select email option to have CIP entry send to you	Email	
6	Attach files, if any		Optional

APPENDIX
H
CIP SUBMISSION
TEMPLATE CHECKLIST

No.	Description	Information	Notes
1	Publisher name		
2	Publisher category		
3	Address		
4	City/town/suburb		
5	State		
6	Postcode		
7	Phone contact		
8	Fax contact		
9	Email address		
10	Contact name		
11	Book title		
12	Subtitle		
13	Edition		
14	Imprint		
15	Format 1		
16	ISBN—remove dashes		
17	Retail price		
18	System requirements (eBook/paperback/hardback/loose leaf/cd)		
19	Planned year of publication		
20	Planned month of publication		
21	Authors/contributors listed on the title page e.g. John Smith (author)		

No.	Description	Information	Notes
22	Life dates and middle names of author/contributor		
23	Description of the book		
24	Genre of audience—fiction or nonfiction and children/play/poetry/short stories		
25	Primary audience (general reader, pre-school age, etc.)		
26	Series title		
27	Series numbering		
28	Bibliography/index		
29	Multivolume numbering (information relating to other volumes in this set).		
30	Previously published edition of this work and ISBN		
FORMAT 2			
1	ISBN—remove dashes		
2	Retail price		
3	System requirements (eBook/paperback/hardback/loose leaf/cd		
FORMAT 3			
1	ISBN—remove dashes		
2	Retail price		
3.	System requirements (eBook/paperback/hardback/loose leaf/cd		
4.	Enter comments (any comments or extra information you'd like to add)		
5.	Select email option to have CIP entry sent to you		
6.	Attach files, if any		Optional

APPENDIX

I

DESIGNER QUOTE/ LAYOUT CHECKLIST

Following are suggested steps for obtaining quotes and choosing a designer. The aim is find a designer you can work with, at a price you choose to afford, for the outcome you want to achieve. You may want to produce only a paperback, if so ignore the eBook references. Alternatively, if you want to generate an eBook ignore the paperback references. This is your book to choose how you want to publish and present to your audience.

No.	Summary of issue to be checked	Tick	Comments
1	Submit manuscript to book designer for quoting on manuscript to be provided in the following formats: CreateSpace—PDF Amazon KDP—mobi Smashwords/other eBooks—ePub		
2	Book designer to provide a sample chapter to confirm format.		
3	Accept/reject layout from book designer.		
4	Book designer then to work on entire book (note—you need to ensure sample provided is included in the full version).		

No.	Summary of issue to be checked	Tick	Comments
5	Interior files to comply to requirements listed below: i) CreateSpace • Black and white book MUST be in black and white in *CMYK* (Cyan, Magenta, Yellow Key) black colour process • Colour book must be in *CMYK* colour process • Must be in PDF ii) Kindle • Mobi format for Amazon Kindle • Must meet Kindle guidelines iii) Smashwords/ePub • ePub or MS Word file for Smashwords • Must meet Smashwords/eBook guidelines		
6	Review/approve/decline		
7	Confirm final layout		
8	Review/approve utilising the review checklist in Appendix J – Proofing Checklist for Printing		
9	Save final version with the wording 'FINAL' in the file name. This file will be used to upload to your chosen platforms and will be referred to as the *book interior*.		

APPENDIX
J
PROOFING CHECKLIST FOR PRINTING

Once your manuscript is ready for printing you need to check the proof from the graphic designer. Unfortunately, the conversion of a word document into a design file can see some things change from your original intention. You must closely review the proof. I am a firm believer of paper-based proofreading. Yes, this may mean printing out your 200-page book, but it is worth it. The checklist I have developed is set out below.

No.	Summary of issue to be checked	Tick	Comments
	FRONT COVER AND BACK COVER		
1	Is the book title and author's name correct on the cover and spine?		
2	Confirm trim size and logo		
3	Is the blurb shown on the back cover correct?		
4	Is the ISBN correct and the barcode clear?		
5	Ensure that no price point is showing on the back cover		
	LAYOUT		
6	Does the Table of Contents have the correct chapters and page numbers or updated after all amendments?		
7	Is the information on the imprint page correct?		
8	Are the pages in the proper order and page numbers correct?		
9	Are all images/diagrams included and in proper placement?		
10	Are all fonts correct?		

No.	Summary of issue to be checked	Tick	Comments
11	Are the margins and page alignment(s) correct?		
12	Confirm all names, salutations, addresses, email and web addresses, and telephone numbers are correct		
13	Are running headers/footers both present on every page where you expect them?		
14	Confirm dates wherever used are correct		
15	Are there any missing characters or broken type?		
16	Double check all spelling & punctuation * Use 'find' function on: double full stops (..) double spacing ( ) the word 'error' '#' space comma (,) semicolon comma (;,)		
17	Consistent formatting throughout (including semicolons, colons, quotations, defining terms, etc.)		
18	Does a space need to be inserted between two words that run together?		
19	Do hyperlinks work when you tap on them?		
20	Are there blank pages?		
21	Is Acknowledgements page inserted where it should be?		
	WRAP UP		
22	Confirm all author notes have been read and deleted		
23	Ensure that any update to PDF is reflected in final word version of source documentation or precedents are made in real time		
24	Confirm cover type (gloss, matte, matte finish, etc.)		
25	Confirm the weight and colour of the final paper stock		

APPENDIX

K

EMAIL TEMPLATES RELATED TO BOOK PUBLISHING AND DESIGNING

Following are email templates that I have developed to assist finding the right people to collaborate with. Tweak as you see fit.

K.1 Workload Capacity Request

Dear [Name],

We require a quote and an indication of your timing to assist with the following:

1. Cover design
2. File uploading for CreateSpace, Kindle, and Smashwords

Would you please let me know the information that you need to assess your capacity to assist?

I look forward to your response.

K.2 Work Request for Interior Design

Dear [Name],

We require a quote and an indication of your timing to assist with the [book title] attached. I would like the font to be converted to (INSERT TYPEFACE).

I look forward to your response.

Or

Dear [Name],

We require a quote and an indication of your timing to assist with the following items:

> I would like to add new chapters to [book title].
>
> Change title on cover to [new title].
>
> Update table of contents and back cover blurb to reflect the new chapters.

The new ISBN is [ISBN number]. I will send you the CIP Entry for the imprint page when I have these details.

Could you please review and let me know if you have any questions in the interim?

K.3 Work Request for Exterior Cover Design

Dear [Name],

I would like a book cover to be created for CreateSpace, Kindle, and Smashwords. Blurb is noted below.

[INSERT your blurb here]

Could you please let me know if you would be able to do this and the timing and cost to complete?

If you would like to book in a time to catch up with me on Skype, please let me know so I can arrange a time that suits us both.

I look forward to your response.

K.4 When Amendments are required for the Exterior Cover Design

Dear [Name],

Thank you for your work on this task.

Please find attached comments for amendments.

For ease of reference these are also listed below:

1.
2.
3.

Please provide CreateSpace draft cover version so we can confirm the back details.

If you could please advise cost and anticipated timing from here.

I look forward to your response.

K.5 Follow-Up on Work Status

Dear [Name],

I have not received a response from you since the below email.

Could you please reply back and let me know the status of this book?

I look forward to your response.

K.6 Reassign Task

(If the quality of the work and the timing of the project is not tracking as you would like it to, a potential option is to email the below, assuming that you are not able to speak directly with this person—phone calls are always first option.)

Dear [Name],

Thank you again for your time and energy with our books.

I will be assigning the [new book/task] to you in a few weeks. To keep other things moving along, we will look after the [old book/task] in the interim.

Please let me know if you have any questions.

APPENDIX

L

BOOK EXTERIOR PRE-PUBLICATION CHECKLIST

No.	Summary of issue to be checked	Tick	Comments
1	If you want to self-design the book cover, minimum requirements are listed below: i) CreateSpace • Cover Must be in *CMYK* colour process • Must be in *PDF* format with properly formatted for particular printers • Check *CreateSpace* guidelines ii) Amazon KDP • Cover Must be in *RGB* (Red, Green, Blue) colour process • Cover should be formatted to 1563 x 2500px (*pixels*) iii) Smashwords/eBook • Cover must be in *RGB* colour process • Cover should be formatted to 1600 x 2400px		
2	Spine will need to be corrected based on interior file final width; this is why the cover needs to be finalised after the interior is confirmed.		
3	No price point on cover. (This is my personal preference, particularly when working in multiple currencies and on multiple platforms. Having a price on your cover can be confusing for the consumer).		
4	Request a 3D (three-dimensional) image of the book cover for promotional use while books are in production (these look fantastic).		

No.	Summary of issue to be checked	Tick	Comments
5	Review/approve and check if there is any formatting to be fixed here.		
6	Once proof is okay, save final version with the wording 'FINAL' in the file name. This is file to be uploaded with your book interior to your chosen platforms.		

APPENDIX
M
PLATFORM DISTRIBUTION CHECKLIST

Each platform has its own rules and regulations about what you can and cannot do, and how to do it. Personally, I use *Amazon's CreateSpace* and *Kindle* platforms, as well as *Smashwords*, *Lightning Source*, local printers, and my own websites. My personal preferences may not be your own. The processes for each platform are similar. You will need to meet the requirements of the platform you choose.

No.	Summary of issue to be checked	Tick	Comments

1	Upload completed book
	
	   i) CreateSpace (and Lightning Source)
	       • Complete info such as book category, price, volume number, publishing date, etc.
	
	  ii) Amazon KDP (Kindle Direct Publishing)
	       • Must meet Kindle guidelines.
	       Complete info such as book category, price, volume number, publishing date, etc.
	
	  iii) Smashwords
	       • Complete info such as book category, price, volume number, publishing date, etc.		

2	Review/approve.		
3	Record details of links so you can use on your website and other social media.		
4	Update *Author Page* each time a new book or edition is published.		
5	Order copies from CreateSpace/Printer		

No.	Summary of issue to be checked	Tick	Comments
6	Track book order.		
7	Final versions of interior/exterior design to be stored on hard drive and backed up to cloud or back up hard drive.		

APPENDIX
N
MORE LEGAL BITS CHECKLIST

No.	Summary of issue to be checked	Tick	Comments
1	Copy or move a final version of the book interior and exterior to *DropBox* (or other back-up platform). I save my final copies in a number of places, including *DropBox*, *Basecamp* and onto a hard drive. In *Basecamp* I set up a new folder with the final files for easier referencing and to reduce the likelihood of uploading a previous version (Yes, I have learnt the hard way with this.) While reloading files is relatively easy, it is time-consuming and not good for your sanity.		
2	ISBN input via *My Identifiers*		
3	EBook legal deposit		
4	Legal deposit with your State Library—refer to Appendix O.		
5	Legal deposit with the National Library of Australia—refer to Appendix P.		
6	Lodge book for *Copyright* (this is not a legal requirement, however highly recommended). http://www.copyright-australia.com/		

APPENDIX

O

LEGAL DEPOSIT LETTER— STATE/TERRITORY

This template letter is standardised for the state of Queensland, however you can change to the state or territory that is relevant to you.

Letter to Queensland State Library

PO Box 1234
New Place Qld 4000

[DATE]
Legal Deposit (Queensland)
Discovery
State Library of Queensland
PO Box 3488
South Brisbane QLD 4101

Dear State Library of Queensland,

Legal Book Deposit

Please find enclosed the following paperback for your recording:

1. BOOK NAME here—ISBN here

Thank you for your assistance.

Yours sincerely,
Jo Jones
Director
D&M Smith (Publishing House)

APPENDIX

P

LEGAL DEPOSIT LETTER— NATIONAL LIBRARY OF AUSTRALIA

Template Letter to National Library of Australia

PO Box 1234
New Place Qld 4000

[DATE]
Legal Deposit Unit
National Library of Australia
Canberra ACT 2600

Dear National Library of Australia,

Legal Book Deposit

Please find enclosed the following paperback for your recording:

1. BOOK NAME here—ISBN here

Thank you for your assistance.

Yours sincerely,
Jo Jones
Director
D&M Smith (Publishing House)

APPENDIX

Q

EDEPOSIT SUBMISSION SAMPLE

No.	Description	Information	Notes
1	Contact Name	Jo Jones	Who is the best person for the eDeposit registrar to contact if there is an issue?
2	Email Address	jo@jones.com	
3	Phone Number	12345678	
4	Institute	D&M Smith	Your publishing house or your name
5	Type of object to be submitted	Legal Deposit Monographs	Default
6	Book title		
7	Year of publication		
8	Place of publication	New South Wales	Your state
9	Publisher	D&M Smith	Your publishing house or your name
10	Organisation name		Does not apply
11	Author	Jo Jones	As per the ISBN application
12	Description		Use the blurb on the back cover
13	Keyword		Use keywords in the description
14	Web address (URL)	http://www. yoursite.com.au/	If you have a website
15	Your name	Jo Jones	
16	Your email address	Jo@Jones.com	

No.	Description	Information	Notes
17	Contact detail	P.O. Box 1234, New Place QLD 4000, Phone: 12345678	
18	Access rights	Select 'Open Access'	
19	Copyright statement	Select the 'I accept the term'	
20	Upload the file	PDF (under 25 MB)	Note the file size and format. You may need to compress your files if they are over the 25MB limit.
21	Label the file		
22	Add notes		Optional
23	Review and confirm information		

APPENDIX

R

EDEPOSIT SUBMISSION
TEMPLATE CHECKLIST

This template is to assist you to gather sufficient information and data before you try to input your eBook to save you time in processing.

No.	Description	Information	Notes
1	Contact name		
2	Email address		
3	Phone number		
4	Institute		
5	Type of object to be submitted		
6	Book title		
7	Year of publication		
8	Place of publication		
9	Publisher		
10	Organisation name		
11	Author		
12	Description		
13	Keyword		
14	Web address (URL)		
15	Your name		
16	Your email address		
17	Contact detail		
18	Access rights		
19	Copyright statement		
20	Upload the file		

No.	Description	Information	Notes
21	Label the file		
22	Add Notes		
23	Review and confirm information		

APPENDIX

S

MARKETING CHECKLIST

No.	Summary of issue to be checked	Tick	Comments
1	Draft updates for social media websites • Twitter • Blog • MailChimp		
2	Review/approve.		
3	Book to be sent to website content manager • Front cover only in JPEG (300 dpi) • Full PDF of book		
4	Website Content Manager to arrange book covers, to be uploaded to website with links to: • CreateSpace • Amazon KDP • Smashwords		
5	Website Content Manager to arrange: • Free PDF download hidden page on your website		
6	Upload order forms		
7	Consider 'Sales Day' (e.g. all books 50% off).		

APPENDIX
T
BASECAMP TRAINING MANUAL AND TEMPLATE SAMPLES

I have been using Basecamp for over a decade for my entire project management needs. Personally, I love it. You can Google Basecamp (and similar platforms) for reviews and specifications. I have created my templates in Basecamp to mirror my checklists and process flowchart.

The summary set out below is extracted from Basecamp's website and you can review the links to see what they are about if you are not familiar with them.

Basecamp

What is Basecamp?

Basecamp is a web-based project management tool that helps you manage multiple projects at a time with to-do lists, file sharing, conversations, calendars, and time tracking. If you are new to Basecamp, please watch these recommended videos to help you get started:

I've just been invited to Basecamp (45 seconds)
https://basecamp.com/help/videos/welcome

Basecamp Help Guide (general search and find page)
https://basecamp.com/help

Organise Your To-do Items (45 seconds)
https://basecamp.com/help/videos/organizing-to-dos

Subscribing to Your Basecamp Calendars (1 minute and 11 seconds)
https://basecamp.com/help/videos/subscribe-to-your-calendars

Saving Time with Project Templates (1 minute and 19 seconds) https://basecamp.com/help/videos/project-templates

How to Add Content to Basecamp Project via Email (1 minute)
https://basecamp.com/help/guides/projects/email-in

Basecamp Templates

I realise that I must sound like a Basecamp weirdo, and no, Jason Fried does not know that I am writing about his business. It is difficult to articulate the profound impact having an outstanding online project management tool like Basecamp can be. The ability to know that you have one of the world's leading innovative companies looking after you with a team of amazing people … no more needs to be said.

As I mentioned, I utilise Basecamp to replicate my checklists. If you would like to use Basecamp, the following template may assist you. If you do not intend to use Basecamp, skip this section.

To-Do Lists

1) Manuscript Development

Source from Upwork (formerly Elance) or other similar provider.

Set up project folder to work with contractor.

2) Graphic design interior

CreateSpace

Kindle—mobi file

Smashwords—PDF file

Smashwords/eBooks—ePub file

3) Graphic design exterior

CreateSpace

Kindle

Smashwords

4) Distribution platforms (sample list could be as follows)

Upload book to CreateSpace

Upload book to Kindle

Upload book to Smashwords/Oyster Program

5) Note details of your book links on your chosen platform

Centralise the links for your books onto your project management tool or in a folder on your computer for easy referencing.

6) Order copies of book

Order copies

Input in diary when books are due to arrive

7) Move final version of interior/exterior

Move files to final version folder

Move files to Dropbox

8) Legal deposit and ISBN tracking

ISBN input for all versions eBook

Legal deposit for eBook

Legal deposit to state library of your state

Legal deposit to Australian National Library Canberra

9) Update social media website

Twitter

Blog

MailChimp

10) Book cover to be sent to website update person

Front cover only in JPEG in 1800px x 2700px

Full PDF of book

11) **Website updates** www.yourwebsite.com.au

Book links to CreateSpace

Book links to Amazon

Book link to Smashwords (or whatever platforms you have chosen)

Hidden page with Free PDF version of the Book

APPENDIX

U

SAMPLE TO-DO LIST OR TIMELINE FOR ACTIONS SUMMARY

BOOK PUBLISHING TO-DO LIST SUMMARY

For those who are not interested in an online project management tool, perhaps a table or checklist of key steps is more useful.

Below is a sample of a timeline or to-do list to keep you on track with where you are at, or more importantly, where you need to be. This can assist in keeping you motivated and on task to complete (ship) your book in a timely manner.

Remember, your goal is to independently publish your book. This table is not exhaustive or compulsory.

Task list for your book	Follow up Date	Resource Name	Due Date
Set time line of tasks e.g. complete this table!			
Set one hour per day, every day, to work on the book until it is shipped.			
Collate potential content from existing resources that you have created.			
Finalise manuscript into a format that can be sent to an editor.			
Find an editor			
Send to editor			

Task list for your book	Follow up Date	Resource Name	Due Date
Note comments from the editor and accept or reject as you see fit—this is your book.			
Further editing/ Proofreading			
Obtain ISBN for your book			
Find a graphic designer			
Send to graphic designer			
Note comments from the designer and accept or reject as you see fit— this is your book. (See a pattern here.)			
Confirm final design			
Upload book to platforms			
Finish off the legal bits			
Order copies of books			
Send book for legal deposit			
Market book			

Final Word of Thanks

Thank you for reading to the final page. This is your beginning page. You have created your story to share with others. You have chosen your own way and in your own style. You have done this. Maybe you can help or inspire someone else to bake their (business) book!

Acknowledgments

People who have collaborated and inspired this book are as follows:

My family – immediate, extended and in-laws
Virtualplicity
Dedicated Book Designs
Otto Dimitrijevics
InHouse Publishing
Brian and Moira Andrew
Emma MacTaggart
Jacque Duffy
Upwork
Basecamp
Jesse Transcriptions

James Patterson
Stephen Covey
Betty Edwards
Woman's Weekly Recipe Books

Each time I read a book I take a little bit away and store it in my mind for later retrieval. All that storing has come together in this book.

Thank you to those who have chosen to share their stories in print so that I can learn from you.

"We are what we repeatedly do" –Aristotle

About the Author

Dyan is passionate about collaborating with entrepreneurs to select, organise and take care of their diverse, accomplished and valuable experiences into a compelling, multi-platform, independently published book.

In her work as Creative Director for 'Words From Daddy's Mouth', she knows first-hand what it is like to pull the best bits of many and varied experiences into unique and passionate stories.

As a country girl beginning life in rural Victoria and NSW, you can probably imagine the gorgeous surrounds, quirky people and outdoor adventures that dotted the landscape of her early years. A fascination with people and their vast potential followed her through a science degree in Brisbane, Australia extending into two decades of banking and finance, travel adventures, family creation and business development.

Beginning in the independent publishing industry can be daunting. Coming to understand the multiple facets of the publishing industry has been incredibly fascinating to Dyan. However, as a writer (and entrepreneur), these aspects can seem redundant (and boring). This can stop writers from achieving publication of a book. Dyan has always enjoyed collaborating to realise writer's (and entrepreneur's) dreams. So whether you are interested in the technical aspects of publishing, or you simply want to write a book on your expertise, she collaborates in a way that results in the best outcome for you.

Dyan specialises in bringing entrepreneur's business stories to print. Simply put – Getting it Done.

National Library of Australia Cataloguing-in-Publication

Creator: Burgess, Dyan, author, illustrator.

Title: Bake a (business) Book / Dyan Burgess.

ISBN: 978-1-92540-619-1 (paperback)

ISBN: 978-1-92540-620-7 (ebook: Kindle)

ISBN: 978-1-92540-621-4 (ebook: epub)

Subjects: Self-publishing—Australia—Handbooks, manuals, etc.
               Publishers and publishing—Australia.
               Entrepreneurship.

Other Creators/Contributors: Dedicated Book Services, book designer.

Dewey Number: 070.593

When reviewing could you please mention:

website www.dyanburgess.com

While the author has made every effort to provide accurate Internet addresses at the time of publication, neither the author nor the publisher assumes responsibility for errors, or changes that occur after publication. Further the publisher does not have any control over and does not assume any responsibility for author or third-party websites or their content.

Published by D & M Fancy Pastry Pty Ltd in 2016

Typefaces: Myriad Pro

www.ingramcontent.com/pod-product-compliance
Lightning Source LLC
Chambersburg PA
CBHW052111230326
41599CB00055B/5636